D1305665

ACE YOUR ANIMAL SCIENCE PROJECT

Titles in the
ACE YOUR BIOLOGY SCIENCE PROJECT series:

Ace Your Animal Science Project:
Great Science Fair Ideas

ISBN-13: 978-0-7660-3220-0
ISBN-10:   0-7660-3220-5

Ace Your Exercise and Nutrition
Science Project:
Great Science Fair Ideas

ISBN-13: 978-0-7660-3218-7
ISBN-10:   0-7660-3218-3

Ace Your Human Biology
Science Project:
Great Science Fair Ideas

ISBN-13: 978-0-7660-3219-4
ISBN-10:   0-7660-3219-1

Ace Your Plant Science Project:
Great Science Fair Ideas

ISBN-13: 978-0-7660-3221-7
ISBN-10:   0-7660-3221-3

Ace Your Science Project
About the Senses:
Great Science Fair Ideas

ISBN-13: 978-0-7660-3217-0
ISBN-10:   0-7660-3217-5

ACE YOUR BIOLOGY SCIENCE PROJECT

ACE YOUR ANIMAL SCIENCE PROJECT

Robert Gardner,
David Webster,
Kenneth G. Rainis,
and
Barbara Gardner Conklin

GREAT SCIENCE FAIR IDEAS

E **Enslow Publishers, Inc.**
40 Industrial Road
Box 398
Berkeley Heights, NJ 07922
USA

http://www.enslow.com

Library of Congress Cataloging-in-Publication Data

Ace your animal science project : great science fair ideas / Robert Gardner . . . [et al.].
    p. cm. — (Ace your biology science project)
    Includes bibliographical references and index.
    Summary: "Presents several science projects and science project ideas about animals"—
        Provided by publisher.
    ISBN-13: 978-0-7660-3220-0
    1. Animal behavior—Experiments—Juvenile literature. 2. Zoology projects—Juvenile literature.
        3. Science projects—Juvenile literature. I. Gardner, Robert, 1929–
    QL751.5A34 2009
    590.78—dc22

                              2008004234

ISBN-10: 0-7660-3220-5

Printed in the United States of America

10 9 8 7 6 5 4 3 2 1

To Our Readers: We have done our best to make sure all Internet Addresses in this book were active and appropriate when we went to press. However, the author and the publisher have no control over and assume no liability for the material available on those Internet sites or on other Web sites they may link to. Any comments or suggestions can be sent by e-mail to comments@enslow.com or to the address on the back cover.

♻ Enslow Publishers, Inc., is committed to printing our books on recycled paper. The paper in every book contains 10% to 30% post-consumer waste (PCW). The cover board on the outside of each book contains 100% PCW. Our goal is to do our part to help young people and the environment too!

Experiments in this book are a collection of the authors' best experiments, which were previously published by Enslow Publishers, Inc. in *Crime-Solving Science Projects: Forensic Science Experiments*, *Health Science Projects About Psychology*, *Microscope Science Projects and Experiments: Magnifying the Hidden World*, and *Science Project Ideas About Animal Behavior*.

Illustration Credits: Courtesy Neo/SCI Corporation, Rochester, NY, Figures 3, 7; Jacob Katari, Figures 1, 2, 11–24, 29; Kenneth G. Rainis, Figures 4–6, 8–10; Stephen F. Delisle, Figures 25–28, 30, Table 1.

Photo Credits: © 2008 Jupiterimages Corporation, p. 3 (boy); © David Lochhead/iStockphoto.com, p. 48; Shutterstock, pp. 1, 3 (animals), 12, 64.

Cover Photos: © 2008 Jupiterimages Corporation (boy); Shutterstock (animals).

CONTENTS

⊙ *Indicates experiments that offer ideas for science fair projects.*

Studying Human Behavior 87

◉ *Indicates experiments that offer ideas for science fair projects.*

INTRODUCTION

When you hear the word *science*, do you think of a person in a white lab coat surrounded by beakers of bubbling liquids, specialized lab equipment, and computers? What exactly is science? Maybe you think science is only a subject you learn in school. Science is much more than this.

Science is the study of the things that are all around you, every day. No matter where you are or what you are doing, scientific principles are at work. You don't need special materials, equipment, or even a white lab coat to be a scientist. Materials commonly found in your home, at school, or at a local store will allow you to become a scientist and pursue an area of interest. By making careful observations and asking questions about how things work, you can begin to design experiments to investigate a variety of questions. You can do science. You probably already have but just didn't know it!

Perhaps you are reading this book because you are looking for an idea for a science fair project for school, or maybe you are just hoping to find something fun to do on a rainy day. This book will provide an opportunity to conduct experiments and collect data to learn more about animals. Animals vary in many ways, including shape, size, habitat, and behavior. The study of animals is called zoology, and scientists who study animals are called zoologists. Would you like to become a zoologist?

SCIENCE FAIR PROJECT IDEAS

Many of the experiments in this book may be appropriate for science fair projects. These experiments are marked with a symbol (⬇) and include a section called Science Fair Project Ideas. The ideas in this section will provide suggestions to help you develop your own original science fair project. However, judges at such fairs do not reward projects or experiments that are simply copied from a book. For example, a model of a bee, which is commonly found at these fairs, would probably not impress judges unless it was done in a novel way. On the other hand, a carefully performed experiment to find out how temperature affects fish respiration would be likely to receive careful consideration.

THE SCIENTIFIC METHOD

All scientists look at the world and try to understand how things work. They make careful observations and conduct research about a question. Different areas of science use a number of different approaches. Depending on the phenomenon being investigated, one method is likely to be more appropriate than another. Designing a new medication for heart disease, studying the spread of an invasive plant species, such as purple loosestrife, and finding evidence that there was once water on Mars all require different methods.

Despite the differences, however, all scientists use a similar general approach to do experiments. It is called the scientific method. In most experiments, some or all of the following steps are used: making an observation, formulating a question, making a hypothesis (an answer to the question) and prediction (an if-then statement), designing and conducting an experiment, analyzing results, drawing conclusions, and accepting or rejecting the hypothesis. Scientists then share their findings with others by writing articles that are published in journals. After—and only after—a hypothesis has repeatedly been supported by experiments can it be considered a theory.

You might be wondering how to get an experiment started. When you observe something in the world, you may become curious and think of a question. Your question can be answered by a well-designed investigation. Your question may also arise from an earlier experiment or from background reading. Once you have a question, you should make a hypothesis. Your hypothesis is a possible answer to the question (what you think will happen). Once you have a hypothesis, it is time to design an experiment.

In most cases, it is appropriate to do a controlled experiment. This means there are two groups treated exactly the same except for the single factor that you are testing. That factor is often called a variable. For example, if you want to investigate whether green plants need light, two groups may be used. One group is called the control group, and the other is called the experimental group. The two groups of plants should be treated exactly the same: They should receive the same amount and type of soil and water, be kept at the same temperature, and so forth. The control group will be put in the dark while the experimental group will be put in the light. The variable is light—it is the thing that changes—and it is the only difference between the two groups.

During the experiment, you will collect data. For example, you might measure growth of the plants in centimeters, or count the number of dead leaves. You might note color and condition of the leaves. By comparing the data collected from the control group with the data collected from the experimental group, you will draw conclusions. Since the two groups were treated exactly alike, increased growth of plants in the light would allow you to conclude with confidence that more growth is a result of the one thing that was different: light being available to the plant.

Two other terms that are often used in scientific experiments are *dependent* and *independent* variables. One dependent variable here is growth, because growth depends upon light availability. Light is the independent variable (it doesn't depend on anything). After the data is collected, it is analyzed to see whether the hypothesis was supported or rejected. Often, the results of one experiment will lead you to a related question, or they may send you off in a different direction. Whatever the results, there is something to be learned from all scientific experiments.

SCIENCE FAIRS

Science fair judges tend to reward creative thought and imagination. It helps if you are really interested in your project. Take the time to choose a topic that really appeals to you. Consider, too, your own ability and the cost of materials. Don't pursue a project that you can't afford.

If you decide to use a project found in this book for a science fair, you will need to find ways to modify or extend it. This should not be difficult because you will probably find that as you do these projects new ideas for experiments will come to mind. These new experiments could make excellent science fair projects, particularly because they spring from your own mind and are interesting to you.

If you decide to enter a science fair and have never done so before, you should read some of the books listed in the Further Reading section. The books that deal specifically with science fairs will provide plenty of helpful hints and lots of useful information that will enable you to avoid the pitfalls that sometimes plague first-time entrants. You will learn how to prepare appealing reports that include charts and graphs, how to set up and display your work, how to present your project, and how to relate to judges and visitors.

SAFETY FIRST

As with many activities, safety is important in science, and certain rules apply when conducting experiments. Some of the rules below may seem obvious to you, while others may not, but each is important to follow.

1. Have **an adult** help you whenever the experiment advises.

2. Wear eye protection and closed-toe shoes (rather than sandals), and tie back long hair.

3. Don't eat or drink while doing experiments, and never taste substances being used.

4. Avoid touching chemicals.

5. Keep flammable substances away from fire.

6. When doing these experiments, use only non-mercury thermometers, such as those filled with alcohol. The liquid in some thermometers is mercury. It is dangerous to breathe mercury vapor. If you have mercury thermometers, **ask an adult** to take them to a local mercury thermometer exchange location.

7. When using a microscope, always use indirect lighting when illuminating objects. Never use the microscope mirror to capture direct sunlight. Because the mirror concentrates light rays, you could permanently damage your eyes.

8. Do only those experiments that are described in the book or those that have been approved by **an adult**.

9. Never engage in horseplay or play practical jokes.

10. Before beginning, read through the entire experimental procedure to make sure you understand all instructions, and clear all items from your work space.

11. At the end of every activity, clean all materials used and put them away. Wash your hands thoroughly with soap and water.

Chapter 1

Animals and Animal Behavior

THERE IS GREAT VARIETY IN THE ANIMAL KINGDOM.
Animals come in many shapes and sizes, and they live in a variety of
habitats, from desert to ocean to tundra. Animals have different diets,
move in different ways, and have a multitude of special features.
Because there are so many differences, it is a challenge to define *animal*.
In many science textbooks, *animal* is defined using a list of criteria or
characteristics that all animals share. Animals may be described as
living things that cannot make their own food the way plants do.
Instead, they need to consume food, by eating plants or other animals
or both. They then convert that food into usable energy. Additionally,
animals move about in their habitats. They can also respond to things
in their environment. All animals share these characteristics.

It is probably easier for you to list the differences between animals
than the similarities. Animal species look different from one another. It is
easy to see that different species have different physical features. Some
animals have feathers, others have scales, and still others have hair.
Some animals produce interesting substances such as silk, which makes up
spider webs, or keratin, which makes up hair and nails. Some animals are
awake in the daytime, while others are active at night. Animals exhibit
all sorts of different behaviors, from burrowing in mud, to flying south for

the winter, to hiding from predators. Many scientists are interested in animal behavior and use a variety of methods to study how animals behave. Humans also belong to the animal kingdom, and their structure, function, and behavior are also of great interest to scientists.

Some people believe that humans represent the most advanced stage of animal evolution. It is true that we can learn to talk, read, write, and reason. We can also pass on what we learn to future generations through books, films, letters, photographs, and many other means. But other animals contribute much to our world. As people have learned more and more about animals, they have gained a greater appreciation for them. There are many things that can be done to better protect animals, especially those that are endangered. Protecting habitats and regulating hunting are ways people can prevent animals from becoming extinct.

Certainly, it is easy to recognize that some animals have skills that are superior to ours. A gazelle, a horse, a bear, and many other animals can run faster than humans can. Most mammals have a much better sense of smell than people do. The eagle's keen eyesight is far better than ours. We can hear only those sounds between 20 and 20,000 vibrations per second, while dogs can hear sounds from 15 to 50,000 vibrations per second. Bats, which use the echoes of sounds to locate their prey, can hear sounds of 1,000 to 120,000 vibrations per second, and dolphins can hear sounds of 150 to 150,000 vibrations per second. Figure 1 is a graph that shows the range of hearing and voice sounds for several different animals.

A dog's ability to hear very high pitched sounds—sounds with more than 20,000 vibrations per second—is the basis for dog whistles. When a dog owner blows such a whistle, people cannot hear it. But a dog can hear these sounds and will respond if properly trained.

Many animals see light that people cannot see. Rattlesnakes can see infrared light, which people can only sense as heat. They use this added range of sight to find their prey at night. Many insects can see ultraviolet light that people cannot detect without the aid of instruments. The insects' ability to see this light helps them find nectar and pollen on flowers that reflect ultraviolet light.

Nocturnal animals—animals that are active at night—have an extra layer of tissue at the very back of their eyes. This layer reflects light

[FIGURE 1]

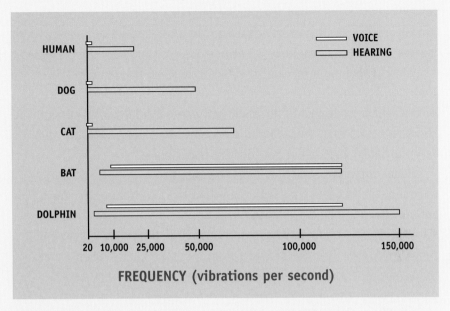

This graph shows the frequency of sounds (the number of vibrations per second) that can be heard and made (voice) by five different animals. As you can see, humans can hear and vocalize a relatively small range of sounds.

through the retina, the membrane that receives the image. Some of the light that was not absorbed as it passed through the retina the first time is absorbed on the second trip. The added light gained by reflection enables cats to see well in the dark. It is this reflected light that makes the eyes of a cat or raccoon glow at night when light strikes their eyes.

While a dog's sense of smell is probably a thousand times better than ours, the sense of smell of fish is a thousand times more sensitive than a dog's. This means that a fish's sense of smell is a million times better than ours.

Salmon, for example, always return to spawn in the same stream in which they hatched. Some scientists believed that the fish use their keen sense of smell to find their way home. To test this idea, a number of salmon were captured in a stream. They were then taken downstream below the fork in the river where they had originally gone to the left. Next, half the salmon had their noses stuffed with cotton. Both groups of salmon—those that could smell and those that could not smell—were marked so that they could be identified. The salmon were then released.

After swimming upstream, they again reached the same fork in the river. The salmon that could smell all chose the left fork again. Of the salmon that could not smell, half chose the left fork and half chose the right fork. This would be expected by chance. Without their sense of smell, they could not identify their "home."

Some organisms—such as birds, whales, and even some bacteria—have built-in magnets that help them find their way along the earth's surface. Homing pigeons released near an iron mine, where there is a strong magnetic field, may have difficulty beginning their homeward flight. They may fly some distance from the mine before turning and flying toward home. If a tiny but strong magnet is attached to a pigeon's body, the magnet interferes with the bird's ability to detect the earth's magnetic field. Nevertheless, on a sunny day pigeons with attached magnets will quickly head for home. On cloudy days, they fly in random directions. This suggests that they can use the sun, as well as the earth's magnetic field, to navigate.

You may think that only humans can communicate, but you've probably seen animals get their message across. A dog can certainly let you know when it wants to go outside. From experience, you know that a dog's wagging tail or a cat's purring shows contentment, while a growl or a hiss indicates dislike or signals a warning. The barking of a watchdog tells its owner that someone or something is approaching, and even a cricket's chirping rate can be used to tell temperature.

TWO WAYS OF KNOWING

All animals are able to respond to stimuli—things that cause a response (action)—and the response may indicate either active or passive knowledge. Active knowledge is knowledge that is learned. Passive knowledge is not learned; it is innate. It consists of responses an animal is born with. Innate responses are built into an animal's nervous system by the genes it receives from its parents.

It is not always easy to decide whether a behavior is caused by active or passive knowledge. If an egg is removed from a goose's nest, the goose will use its bill to roll the egg back into the nest. This would appear to be learned behavior. The goose is acting in a reasonable way to regain an egg that was removed from the nest. However, the behavior is actually innate. It is an inborn response to a stimulus. The response can be triggered by any egg, and it doesn't have to be its own egg. In fact, a goose will roll lightbulbs, baseballs, and even flashlight batteries into its nest. The response seems to be strongest if the object is round, large, green, and spotted—like a goose egg.

Stimuli that trigger such innate responses as egg rolling are called releasers. They cause the animal to "release" the innate behavior stored in its nervous system. Herring gull chicks will peck at their parents' beaks to obtain food. The stimulus that acts as a releaser for this pecking behavior is the horizontal motion of a narrow, vertical, colored object such as a parent bird's beak. (An adult herring gull has a red spot on its beak.) If a narrow wooden dowel (stick) with red stripes is held vertically and moved back and forth, chicks will peck at it the same as they peck at a parent's beak.

If the releaser is a chemical, it is called a pheromone. Many insects use pheromones to attract a mate. Bees have several different phero-mones. One is used to signal an attack on an invader; a second to indicate alarm; a third to attract bees to food; another to identify the queen bee; and so on.

In the case of a goose rolling an egg, the releaser is the sight of an egg or an egglike object outside the nest. Even if the egg is then taken away, the goose behaves in the same way. It goes through the same motions, which shows that the response is an innate behavior.

Interestingly, geese will carry out egg-rolling behavior only while their eggs are being incubated. Once the eggs hatch, a goose will not retrieve an egg or egglike object placed outside the nest.

CONDITIONED LEARNING

About one hundred years ago, Ivan Pavlov, a Russian scientist and Nobel Prize winner, was using dogs to study digestion. He had connected tubes

[FIGURE 2a]

[FIGURE 2b]

BELL

2a) A dog salivates automatically when food is placed in its mouth.
 b) After conditioning, a dog will salivate when it hears the conditioned stimulus (bell, can opener, or whatever it associates with
being fed).

to a dog in order to measure the saliva the dog produced when food was placed in its mouth (see Figure 2a).

Shortly after starting his experiments, Pavlov discovered that the dog would begin to salivate (form saliva) as soon as it heard food being prepared. He then tried ringing a bell before the dog was fed. The dog soon learned that the bell meant food was coming. It would salivate as soon as it heard the bell (see Figure 2b).

Pavlov called this learning process "conditioning." He called whatever was used to make the dog salivate before it received food (the bell or the sound of food being prepared, for example) the conditioned stimulus (CS). The formation of saliva by the dog in response to the bell (or any other CS), Pavlov called the conditioned response (CR).

Food alone was an unconditioned stimulus (US). Food placed in a dog's mouth caused the dog to secrete saliva. In this case, the formation of saliva is an unconditioned response (UR). Like you, a dog will salivate when food is placed in its mouth. Secretion of saliva is an automatic (unconditioned) response to food in the mouth. It is built-in (innate) behavior for both humans and dogs.

A lot of animal and human learning takes place through trial-and-error conditioning. We keep trying a number of things until something works. When it works, we repeat it because it provides the result we want. Learning how to ride a bicycle or hit a baseball are examples of trial-and-error learning. However, good coaching can help us to eliminate many of the errors we might otherwise make. In the experiment that follows, you will learn how to condition your dog.

Materials:

- dog
- stimulus, such as a bell, glass and spoon, or whistle

If you have a dog, it may already be conditioned. For example, if you use a can opener to open dog food, the sound of the machine may be a conditioned stimulus. If your dog comes to the kitchen when it hears the can opener, it has probably learned that the sound means "dinnertime." It probably salivates (CR) when it hears the can opener (CS).

See if you can condition your dog to another stimulus. Try ringing a bell, whistling a particular tune, tapping a glass with a spoon, or using some other stimulus just before you feed your dog. If the dog is conditioned to another sound, such as the can opener, avoid using that stimulus. Open the can where the dog can't hear you.

Does the new stimulus become a conditioned stimulus for the dog? How long does it take before the dog learns that the stimulus means food is coming?

 ## Science Fair Project Idea

Use conditioning to train your dog to shake hands, sit, stay, heel, roll over, and fetch the paper. Can you train your dog to do these things? What other things can you train your dog to do?

Chapter 2

Variety in the Animal Kingdom

ANIMALS COME IN ALL DIFFERENT SIZES. You may already know that the largest of all animals is the blue whale and that the largest land animal is an elephant. But can you name some of the smallest animals? There are some animals that you have probably never seen because they are so small. In this chapter, you will be able to look at some of the smallest animals and some animal parts, such as feathers and scales, under a microscope.

HENRY BAKER (1698–1774)

Henry Baker was a naturalist, poet, and pioneer of education for the speech and hearing impaired. One of the first historians of the microscope, Henry Baker wrote *The Microscope Made Easy* in 1742. His pioneering work on the hydra, an aquatic invertebrate, helped develop the microscope into the instrument it is today. Working with instrument maker John Cuff (1708–1772), Baker suspended a lens on a horizontal arm above a circular stage. Light was directed through a hole in the stage using a mirror mounted at the base.

Microscopes improve our understanding of how cells work together to form tissues and organs—the stuff of which larger organisms are made. The following section will explain how to use a microscope to look closely at some animals and to answer questions about how animals age, how they obtain food, and how they make and use unique materials. Before continuing, acquaint yourself with parts of a microscope (Figure 3), along with the techniques that follow.

USING A MICROSCOPE

Always use indirect lighting when illuminating objects. Never use the microscope mirror to capture direct sunlight. Because the mirror concentrates light rays, you could permanently damage your eyes.

1. Begin by examining any object using the lowest-power objective. Place a glass slide containing your specimen on the stage with the center of the slide over the hole in the stage, specimen-side up.

2. Adjust the light source (flat mirror surface or illuminator) and iris or disk diaphragm until light passes through the specimen. With the low-power objective in place, use the coarse adjustment knob to move the objective downward until it is about 1/4 inch (0.6 cm) from the surface of the coverslip.

3. Look through the eyepiece and slowly raise the objective with the coarse adjustment knob until the specimen is in approximate focus. Then use the fine adjustment knob to bring the image into sharp focus. Readjust the focus often, using fine focus to view all parts of your specimen.

4. Adjust the disk or iris diaphragm for best lighting. You will need more light (a wider diaphragm opening) at higher magnifications.

5. When rotating higher-power objectives into the optical path, you will feel a click as the objective locks into place. To avoid jamming the objective lens into the slide preparation, sharpen the focus using the fine adjustment knob only. Never focus under high power with the coarse adjustment knob.

6. Never touch lenses.

7. Keep the microscope stage clean and dry. If any liquids are spilled, wipe them up immediately with paper towels.

[FIGURE 3]

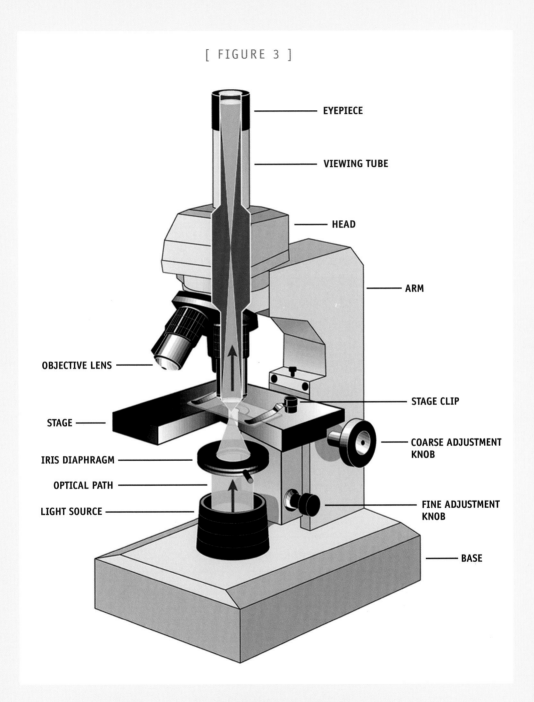

EYEPIECE

VIEWING TUBE

HEAD

ARM

OBJECTIVE LENS

STAGE CLIP

STAGE

COARSE ADJUSTMENT KNOB

IRIS DIAPHRAGM

OPTICAL PATH

LIGHT SOURCE

FINE ADJUSTMENT KNOB

BASE

Compound Microscope Parts

8. Resolution = Information: What you see with increased magnification depends upon the resolution of your scope. Optical resolution is determined by how well the viewing eye can distinguish the individual parts of an object. Most microscope objectives are labeled 4X, 10X, and 40X. Resolution is greatest at 40X, while size and depth of field (the zone that is in focus) are greatest at 4X.

9. To determine how greatly magnified the field of view is, multiply the number inscribed on the eyepiece lens by the number on the objective being used. For example:

   eyepiece (5X) × objective (4X) = total magnification (20X)

10. To estimate the size of your field of view, secure a 1-inch-square piece of 1-mm-ruled graph paper to a glass microscope slide and center it in the field of view. Make sure that one edge just touches the outer rim of the field. Since the distance between ruled lines is 1 mm (1,000 μm), the size of the field for your microscope can be estimated.

In general, the following field sizes are good estimates for a microscope having a 10X eyepiece.

	Objective	*Size of Field*
10X	low-power objective	1,600 μm
43X	high dry objective	375 μm
100X	oil-immersion objective	160 μm

MEASURING THINGS

Scientists use a system of measurement known as the International System of Units, or SI, based upon the metric system. The metric system uses multiples of 10 and is based upon a standard length of 1 meter, a standard volume of 1 liter, and a standard mass of 1 kilogram. Micrometer (μm) is a standard unit of measure often used in microscopy.

SI Conversion Table		
SI Unit (Length)	*From SI to Customary*	*From Customary to SI*
kilometer (km) = 1,000 m	1 km = 0.621 miles (mi)	1 mi = 1.609 km
meter (m) = 100 cm	1 m = 3.281 feet (ft)	1 ft = 0.305 m
centimeter (cm) = 0.01 m	1 cm = 0.394 inch (in)	1 in = 2.54 cm
millimeter (mm) = 0.001 m	1 mm = 0.039 inch (in)	
micrometer (μm) = 0.000001 m		
nanometer (nm) = 0.000000001 m		

MICROTECHNIQUES

Microtechniques are ways of preparing specimens for microscopic observation. These techniques will help you get the most out of your time with the microscope.

Use care when working with stains. Avoid skin and eye contact. Wear eye and hand protection.

MAKING A WET MOUNT

This microtechnique is useful for preparing a sample to be viewed under the microscope.

Using an eyedropper, place a drop of water in the center of a clean microscope slide. Transfer the sample you wish to mount to the drop of water on the microscope slide.

Carefully add a coverslip to make a wet-mount preparation of the sample. To avoid air bubbles, slowly lower the coverslip at an angle on the drop so that air bubbles do not form on the slide.

If the sample is too thick, you may need to add a small drop of water under the coverslip. Place the prepared slide on the stage of a compound microscope.

MOVING SOLUTIONS

This microtechnique is useful for introducing a stain or another solution to microscopic life-forms or cells under a coverslip in a wet mount.

Cut or tear a triangular piece of paper towel. Use an eyedropper to place a drop of stain or solution on one side of the coverslip, so that it just mixes with the existing fluid of the wet mount. Carefully insert one point of the paper towel piece underneath the opposite side of the coverslip. Watch as the liquid moves from one side of the coverslip to the other.

You may need to place additional drops of stain or use another paper towel piece to complete the introduction of stain or another solution under the coverslip (see Figure 4).

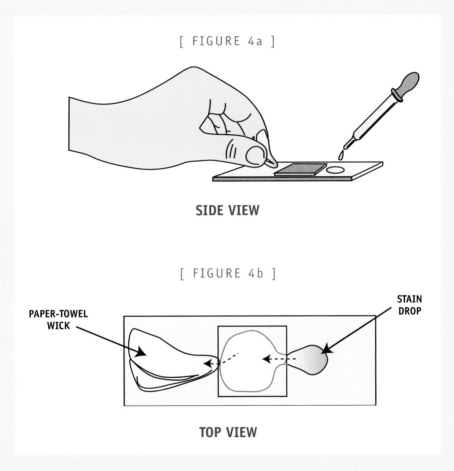

SIDE VIEW

PAPER-TOWEL
WICK

STAIN
DROP

TOP VIEW

Moving solutions. a) Add a drop of the solution you want to introduce.
b) Use a paper-towel wick to replace one solution with another.

STAINING

This microtechnique is useful for adding contrast to transparent organisms and tissues. You may need this technique for a science fair project. **Safety: Use care when working with stains. Avoid skin and eye contact. Wear eye and hand protection.**

Most living tissues and microorganisms are transparent, so adding contrast (a range of color) can help you see an object. Good contrast allows for the observation of fine detail at a particular magnification.

Obtain biological stains from your science teacher or other adult. Loeffler's methylene blue stain (0.1 percent) or iodine (one drop mixed with a drop of water on a slide) is excellent for adding contrast to most transparent biological materials. Crystal violet stain (0.1 percent) is also excellent for staining bacteria.

In a pinch you can use food coloring. Mix one drop food coloring with one drop of water on a slide.

Materials:
-kitchen baster
-water samples in separate plastic containers
-microscope slides
-plastic coverslips
-eyedropper
-compound microscope, with light source

Rotifers, or "wheel animals," were first described in 1702 by the great microscopist Antoni van Leeuwenhoek in a letter to the Royal Society in London. His description —"two little wheels, which displayed a swift rotation"— sparked the name. Rotifers occur in an endless variety of microhabitats: ponds and puddles, between damp soil particles, and even on mosses.

There are quite a number of rotifers. Some are encased within sculptured shells; others look like miniature worms that inch along. Still others are master builders: Attached to submerged objects or plants, they construct symmetrical tubes.

A common rotifer is *Philodina*, which is so abundant it can be found in almost any drop of water from a pond, ditch, or gutter. It resembles an inchworm with two rotating wheel organs.

Using a kitchen baster, collect outdoor water samples and place them in collecting containers. **With an adult present**, try sampling from a variety of microhabitats, including standing water in gutters, ditches, or ponds. Examine each water sample by making a wet mount. Use an eyedropper to sample the collection containers. Place a drop of water from each on clean microscope slides. Add coverslips, and examine first under medium (100X) magnification. Use Figure 5 as a guide to rotifers and other small animals. How many kinds can you identify?

Measure the size of a rotifer. Compare its size to that of other micro animals such as hydras, water fleas, and copepods. Which is the smallest animal?

[FIGURE 5]

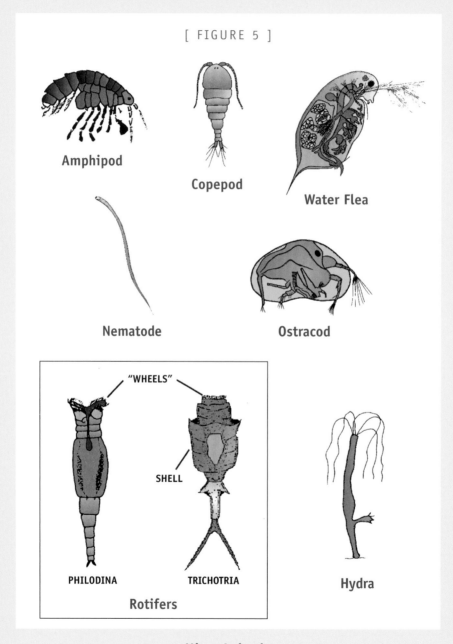

Amphipod

Copepod

Water Flea

Nematode

Ostracod

"WHEELS"

SHELL

PHILODINA

TRICHOTRIA

Rotifers

Hydra

Micro Animals

Science Fair Project Ideas

- Rotifers are also used as fish food, and pet stores usually have vials of dried *Brachionus* eggs for hatching. *Brachionus* ranges in size up to 300 μm—about 1/3 mm. Prepare a micro aquarium so that you can observe the eggs as they develop and hatch. Place a small number of eggs in the sealed aquarium space and observe over time at the scanning (40X) magnification. Write a report on how the hatching process occurs.

- If you have access to a microscope with a camera attached, make a video illustrating rotifer wheel organs.

Materials:

-an adult

-submerged vegetation samples

-jar or shallow pan

-eyedropper

-modeling clay or silicone culture gum

-microscope slide

-plastic coverslip

-compound microscope, with light source

Although hydras are also very small animals, they are quite different from rotifers. Hydras are one of the few commonly observed freshwater coelenterates (soh LEN tuh rayts). Unlike rotifers, coelenterates are animals with tentacles. They are usually plentiful in unpolluted still waters, where they attach to aquatic vegetation, fallen leaves, and submerged stones.

Hydras have five to eight tentacles that vary in length from species to species. They range from colorless to brown; some are even green due to the presence of tiny green protists that live within their bodies.

With an adult present, gather submerged vegetation from unpolluted ponds and other locations. Place the samples in a jar or shallow pan. Overnight, visible hydras will come to the surface, where they can be picked up using an eyedropper. Sometimes it is easier just to transfer a hydra that is clinging to a small piece of material.

Place hydras in a micro aquarium. To construct one, roll a piece of modeling clay or silicone culture gum into a thin rod that is approximately 2.5 cm (1 in) long. Silicone culture gum is an inexpensive material that allows oxygen to pass into the well's interior to prolong organism viability for days. (Silicone culture gum can be purchased from a science supply house. Your teacher may have a catalog you can use.) Carefully shape this strip into a circle in the center of a clean microscope slide. To avoid leaks, be sure to press down so that the clay and the glass form a tight seal. Using an eyedropper, fill the area inside the micro aquarium pocket with your sample. Make sure that no air bubbles are formed when the coverslip is added (see Figure 6).

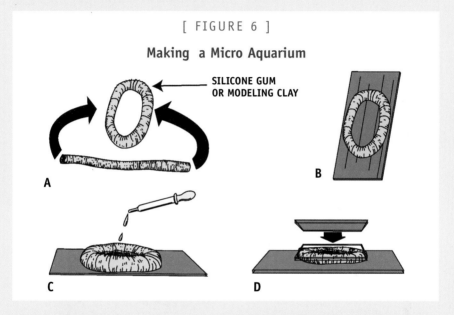

[FIGURE 6]

Making a Micro Aquarium

SILICONE GUM OR MODELING CLAY

A

B

C

D

Micro aquaria and microbes. a) Roll silicone culture gum or clay into a thin rod. b) Form a well on a clean microscope slide; be sure to press down to make a tight seal. c) Use an eyedropper to add a water sample. Continue to add drops until almost overflowing. d) Carefully add a coverslip; avoid creating air pockets.

Place the micro aquarium on the stage and allow the hydra to relax and extend. Using scanning (40X) magnification, observe the body plan of a hydra—a crown of 5 to 8 tentacles atop a long, flexible column. The tentacles contain stinging cells called nematocysts; these surround a mouth that is capable of capturing prey. Hydras use their nematocysts as miniature syringes, injecting a numbing poison into any micro crustacean unlucky enough to brush against its tentacles (see Figure 7).

[FIGURE 7]

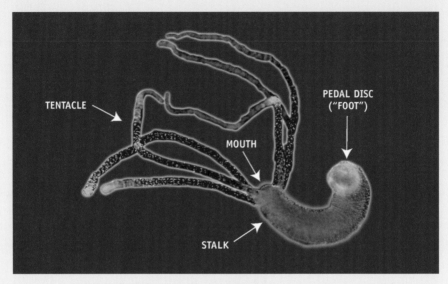

TENTACLE

PEDAL DISC
("FOOT")

MOUTH

STALK

Hydra Anatomy

Science Fair Project Idea

If you have access to a microscope with a camera attached, make a video that shows how hydras feed.

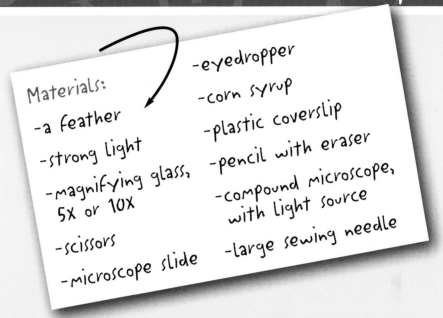

Materials:
- a feather
- strong light
- magnifying glass, 5X or 10X
- scissors
- microscope slide
- eyedropper
- corn syrup
- plastic coverslip
- pencil with eraser
- compound microscope, with light source
- large sewing needle

Feathers help birds fly, and they also trap air, keeping birds warm. Birds regularly use their bills to rearrange, or preen, their feathers. Why do they do this?

Obtain a flight or contour feather. You can find feathers in areas where waterfowl congregate. Use Figure 8 as a guide to feather anatomy. Using your fingers, separate one barb of a contour feather from another barb (pull gently on the outer margin just below the top of the feather). Hold the feather up to a strong light and use your magnifying glass to examine the space between the individual barbs. Note that these spaces are filled with minute structures called barbules that crisscross at opposite angles.

Spread individual barbs on the feather vane. Now run the feather vane back through your fingers (from the bottom toward the top of the feather).

Use scissors to cut a piece of spread feather vane, and make a permanent mount preparation. Place the feather sample in the center of a clean microscope slide. Add two or three drops of corn syrup on top of the feather sample. Next, add a coverslip. Finally, use the eraser end of a pencil to push the coverslip down on the slide. Use a compound microscope at medium (100X) magnification to view the barb and barbule structure. The barbules have tiny hooks that allow them to grab and hold barbs together.

Choose a large flight feather and hold the quill (shaft) toward you. Examine it with a magnifying glass. Notice a small hole that allowed the entrance of blood vessels, which nourished the feather during life. Obtain a large sewing needle and gently push it up into the shaft. What do you observe? Is what you find a benefit to the bird?

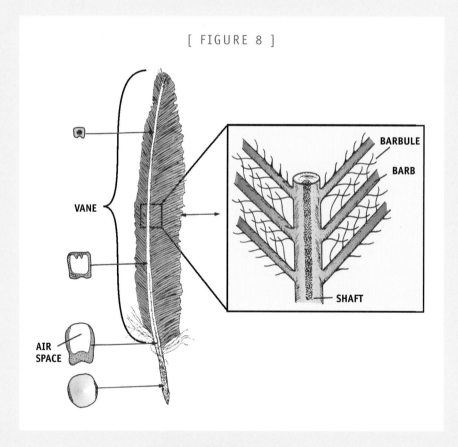

Contour Feather Anatomy

Science Fair Project Ideas

- Take a vegetable peeler and carefully shave the quill of a feather to obtain fine sections (shavings). Use fine tweezers to place a thin section in a drop of water on a microscope slide to make a wet mount. Examine using a compound microscope, and draw what you see in your notebook. If possible, take a fingernail clipping and make a wet mount. Do both appear similar?

- Coloration results from chemical pigments and from the refraction of light through the structural irregularities of the feathers. Red, yellow, brown, and black are due to pigment, and blue and iridescent colors are caused by light refraction. White occurs when no pigment is present and the barbs equally reflect all wavelengths of light. Use a magnifying glass to examine feathers of various colors. Do your observations confirm the above statements?

Materials:
- fish with scales
- tweezers, fine
- microscope slide
- eyedropper
- corn syrup
- plastic coverslip
- pencil with eraser
- compound microscope, with light source

Few fish live longer than twelve years. Most fish that grow longer than 30 cm (1 ft) have a lifespan of at least four or five years, although some fish, such as the sturgeon, can live as long as fifty years.

Fish scales have an exposed portion that you can see and an embedded portion under the skin. There are four main types of fish scales. Most bony fish have ctenoid (rounded; smooth exposed area) or cycloid (oval-shaped; rough exposed area) scales. Others, such as the sturgeon and gar, have ganoid (diamond-shaped) scales. Sharks have placoid (pointed, tooth-shaped) scales. Some catfish and a few other fish species have no scales at all.

You can use Figure 9 as a guide, along with a compound microscope, to determine the age of a fish. If possible, visit the market and obtain some specimens—you can always catch a few fish, too! The ctenoid scales of perch are best to begin with.

Carefully remove scales from the body of a fish using fine tweezers. Allow the scales to dry. Use tweezers to place a dried scale in the center of a clean microscope slide. Use an eyedropper to obtain some corn syrup and place a pea-sized drop directly on the dry specimen. Carefully lay the coverslip down on the drop. Using the eraser end of a pencil, gently spread the drop outward by applying gentle pressure to the center of the coverslip.

Observe this permanent mount first at medium (100X) magnification to identify the scale type. Identify year growth marks, or annuli. They will

[FIGURE 9]

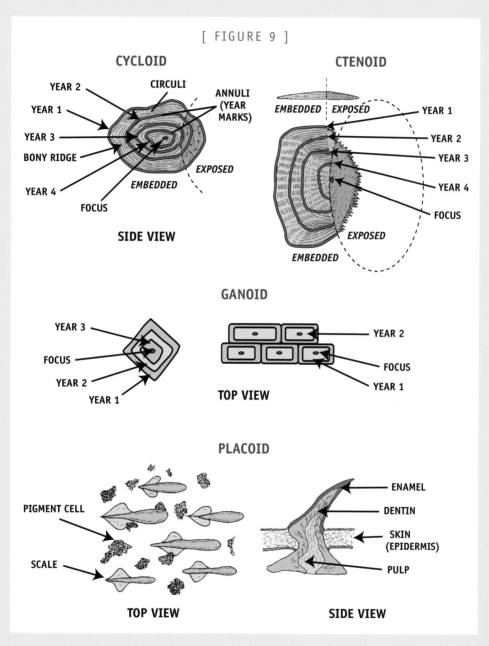

CYCLOID

YEAR 2
CIRCULI
YEAR 1
ANNULI (YEAR MARKS)
YEAR 3
BONY RIDGE
EXPOSED
EMBEDDED
YEAR 4
FOCUS

SIDE VIEW

CTENOID

EMBEDDED | EXPOSED
YEAR 1
YEAR 2
YEAR 3
YEAR 4
FOCUS
EXPOSED
EMBEDDED

GANOID

YEAR 3
FOCUS
YEAR 2
YEAR 1

YEAR 2
FOCUS
YEAR 1

TOP VIEW

PLACOID

PIGMENT CELL
SCALE

TOP VIEW

ENAMEL
DENTIN
SKIN (EPIDERMIS)
PULP

SIDE VIEW

Fish Scale Types

appear as lines around the portion of the scale that grew under the skin. When growth subsides in winter, a very small portion of the scale at the outer edge is absorbed by the fish. As growth begins again in the spring, it leaves a noticeable ring more obvious than the previous ridges. The ringlike markings are called circuli. One annulus (year mark) is formed each year.

Now examine the circuli. They reveal important information about growth periods and environmental and external factors that can affect growth. For example, if overcrowding, reduction of food, or unusually low temperature conditions exist, individual scale ridges will be smaller and closer together. Also look for a lack of scale ridges. These cutoffs indicate a cessation of growth.

You might want to examine several scales from the same fish, since fish often lose scales and the replacements start out with no growth rings.

Science Fair Project Idea

What do you and sharks have in common? Shark scales (placoid scales) are like your teeth—both have a cap of dentin that encloses a pulp cavity and is itself covered by hard enamel (see Figure 9). Fish markets usually carry shark steaks, which still have sharkskin attached. Run your fingers over the skin. Does it feel coarse, like sandpaper? Use a magnifying glass to examine sharkskin closely. You will see the spines of numerous placoid scales embedded in it. Use tweezers, while looking through your lens, to remove several scales. Allow them to dry. Make permanent mounts. Observe them under a compound microscope at medium (100X) magnification.

Materials:
- orb spider web
- eyedropper
- microscope slide
- tweezers, fine
- cuticle scissors
- coverslip
- compound microscope, with light source
- dragline silk

Orb weaver spiders construct the most complicated webs. They weave circular webs in open areas, often between tree branches or flower stems. First, threads of dry silk are laid from the web's center, like the spokes of a wheel. Later, the orb weaver will lay down coiling lines of sticky silk that connect the spokes and serve as the insect trap. When this trapping silk is touched, it adheres to the object touching it. Figure 10 shows how spiders weave their webs.

Ask a local naturalist or nature center how to locate an orb weaver's web. Add a drop of water to a clean microscope slide. Use fine tweezers to hold a small section of coiling line. Use cuticle scissors to cut a section from the web. Make a wet mount by carefully lowering the piece of coiling line to the water drop. Add a coverslip.

Using the microscope, examine the wet mount under 100X magnification. Since spider web material is transparent, increase the contrast by closing the disc or iris diaphragm. Compare your observations to Figure 10. Can you determine which parts of the coiling line are sticky and which are elastic and stretch?

Wherever a spider goes, it spins a silk thread behind itself. This thread is called a dragline. Dragline silk is one of the toughest natural materials known to man. Collect dragline silk and make a wet mount of it. Compare dragline silk to the "dry" and "sticky" silk in an orb weaver's web.

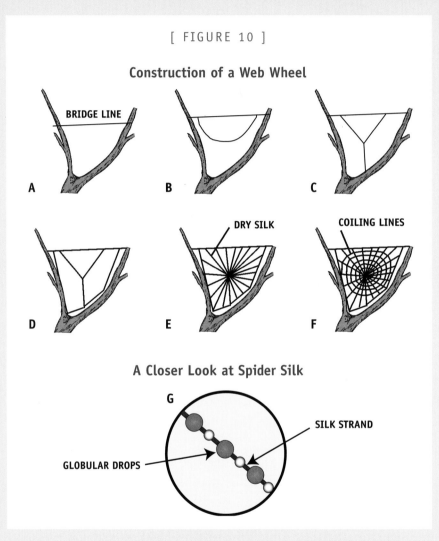

[FIGURE 10]

Construction of a Web Wheel

BRIDGE LINE

A

B

C

DRY SILK

COILING LINES

D

E

F

A Closer Look at Spider Silk

G

SILK STRAND

GLOBULAR DROPS

10a) The orb spider releases a sticky thread that is blown by the wind and carried to a spot where it sticks to form a "bridge line." b) A loose dry thread is then constructed. c) Next, a radius is constructed to make a Y shape. d–e) Additional dry threads are positioned to create a frame and other radii. f) Coiling lines of sticky silk are laid, connecting the spokes to finish the orb web. g) A microscopic look at coiling line shows globular drops on a silk strand.

Science Fair Project Idea

Try comparing dragline and web silks from various spiders such as:

- the grass spider (*Agelena naevia*), which weaves a funnel-shaped web in grass;
- the triangle spider (*Hyptiotes cavatus*), an orb weaver that constructs triangular webs between twigs;
- the common house spider (*Achaearanea tepidariorum*), which constructs a loosely woven tangled web of dry silk held in place by long threads attached to walls and other supports.

Chapter 3

Clever Lab and Field Studies

TRYING TO UNDERSTAND ANIMAL BEHAVIOR IS NOT EASY. Animals can't tell us how they feel, what they think (or if they think), or why they do what they do. They can't talk to us, or at least they don't speak a language that we can understand. Scientists who study animal behavior must design clever experiments to try to find out why animals act the way they do.

This chapter will give you an idea of how a scientist attempts to better understand animals. You will read about some of the experiments that have been done to try to understand animal behavior. Then you can try a couple of experiments on your own.

Many scientists study animals in the field. That is, they observe animals in their natural habitats (where the animals normally live). Other scientists conduct experiments in a laboratory. They bring animals to a laboratory and do experiments there.

In a laboratory, conditions can be controlled. The scientist doesn't have to worry about a predator devouring the animal being studied. Conditions, such as temperature, humidity, length of day, intensity of light, and other factors, can be kept constant or changed at will. On the other hand, removing an animal from its normal environment may change the way it behaves.

A FIELD EXPERIMENT

In the 1950s, J. T. Emlen did a field experiment with cliff swallows. These birds use mud to build nests under cliffs and the eaves of buildings. Unlike most birds, which defend a wide territory around their nests, cliff swallows build their nests next to one another in colonies, as shown in Figure 11. Emlen wondered whether these birds would defend their nests.

Because the swallows looked so much alike, Emlen had to find a way to identify them in his experiment. He crept up close to the colony he was observing. From the top of the cliff, he used a toy water pistol to spray a few drops of quick-drying non-toxic paint on specific birds. He could then use different colors or the different spray patterns to identify them.

Now that he could tell one swallow from another, he saw that the same birds always came to the same nests. They did not share their nests with other swallows. He wondered what would happen if two nests were joined. To find out, he waited until two birds he could identify were away from their adjoining nests. He then removed the wall between the nests. When the birds returned, they fought.

[FIGURE 11]

Cliff swallows build their nests in clusters, but each bird defends only its own nest.

Based on the experiment, Emlen decided that cliff swallows do defend their territory. But unlike most birds, their territory is limited to the nest itself. Once the swallows rebuilt the wall, the fighting stopped.

Many people have used binoculars to watch ground-nesting plovers. These birds will draw attention to themselves in order to protect their eggs or nesting young from predators. Their behavior would make us believe that they are thinking as they draw predators away from their nests.

Sensing a threat, a plover will move slowly away from its eggs or young. If the threat continues, the plover will do one of several things. It may move through the grass, making squeaks that sound like a mouse. It may pretend to be sitting on a nest far from the real nest. When the invader draws near, the bird will fly away, leaving the false nest for the predator to examine. (Its flight will always be away from the real nest in case the predator chooses to chase the plover.) It may make loud calls to attract attention to itself if the predator is approaching the nest (see Figure 12). Its most deceptive move is to pretend it has a broken wing and flop around noisily. The predator, sensing the plover is unable to fly, sprints to what it thinks is a quick meal. But just before it reaches the floundering plover, the bird takes flight, always in a direction away from its nest. Its return path to its chicks or eggs is never direct but roundabout.

The plover's behavior may be innate. To an observer, it certainly looks as though the bird is thinking of the best way to keep the predator from finding its nest.

[FIGURE 12]

This plover shows aggressive behavior toward a cow that is close to the bird's on-the-ground nest. The plover fears that the cow will step on the nest.

A LABORATORY EXPERIMENT

Barn owls are valuable to farmers because they eat field mice that feed on orchard and field crops (see Figure 13). These birds are active at night. They usually remain quiet during the daytime. Roger Payne, who has studied many different animals, knew that barn owls feed almost exclusively on field mice. But how do they find their prey in darkness?

Even in daytime, field mice are hard to see because they build grass tunnels that cover their movements. It occurred to Payne that although mice do remain hidden most of the time, they must make noise as they move through their grass tunnels. Could it be that owls use their ears rather than their eyes to find field mice?

To find out, Payne set up an experiment. His laboratory was a large room in an old building. He carefully covered all the windows and cracks with boards, tape, and putty until he was sure that no light, not even bright sunlight, could enter the room. Since he planned to do his experiments at night in a lightproof room, he was certain that an owl could not use its eyes to find its prey. He spread leaves over the floor so that a mouse would make a rustling noise when it moved around the room.

Payne obtained an owl that had always lived in captivity. After the owl had lived in the room a few days, Payne carried out his first experiment. He released a mouse into the dark room. Nothing happened! He turned on the lights, and the owl finally flew to the floor. But it didn't land on the mouse as owls usually do. Instead, it caught the mouse by running after it. Payne thought that because the owl had been raised in captivity, it had never seen its parents catch mice. It would have to learn how to hunt by itself. After a few trials with the lights on, the owl began to land directly on the mouse. Payne decided the owl had learned the proper way to hunt.

In his next experiment, Payne released a mouse into the dark room and waited. For an hour, the mouse barely moved. Then, at last, Payne heard it move slowly through the leaves. Seconds later he heard a thud. He turned on the lights. There was the owl with the mouse in its talons!

An hour later, he repeated the experiment with the same results. The owl, although raised in captivity, had learned to hunt very quickly after a few practice sessions in light. But was the owl really locating mice

[FIGURE 13]

A large part of a barn owl's diet is mice.

with its ears, or did it smell the mouse? Perhaps the owl detected its prey by the heat radiating from the mouse's body. Could the owl, like rattlesnakes, have eyes that can see the infrared light released by warm bodies?

To find out if the owl detected the mouse by sensing heat or odor, Payne repeated the experiment using a cold "mouse." Actually, he used a wad of paper that he pulled along the floor with a string. If the owl was guided by heat or odor, it should not be able to find this cold mouse. Payne had barely started to pull the cold mouse along the floor when— *wham!*—the owl landed on the wad of paper. Payne had shown that the owl did not have to rely on infrared radiation or smell to locate its prey in darkness.

Of course, Payne had not proved that owls do not *use* smell to hunt their prey. He had simply shown that they do not *need* to use smell to find a mouse.

Perhaps the owl, like a bat, was locating its prey by sending out high-pitched sounds and then following the echoes. The echoes from a mouse would have to have a particular characteristic that the owl could recognize. Otherwise, it wouldn't know whether it was flying at a mouse, a lion, or a stone.

To see if the owl was using a sonar system similar to a bat's, Payne used a small loudspeaker to broadcast a recording of a mouse running through leaves. If the owl was using echoes, it would recognize that the sound reflected from the loudspeaker was different than the sound reflected from a mouse. The owl quickly (but disappointedly) landed on the loudspeaker. Obviously, it was not relying on echoes to locate its prey.

In another experiment, Payne placed a dead mouse and a loud-speaker in different places under the leaves. Nothing happened until he turned on the recorded sound. When he did, the owl immediately struck the loudspeaker and ignored the mouse. This experiment strongly suggests that if the owl uses smell to hunt at all, it much prefers to use its hearing.

In a rather conclusive test, Payne used a cotton wad to plug one of the owl's ears. The owl missed the mouse every time. Without full use of both ears, the owl could not find its prey. Payne could now be reasonably sure that the owl was using its ears to locate mice. He repeated this experiment many times with different owls. The results were always the same.

To determine an owl's accuracy in locating mice, Payne tied a dead mouse to the small loudspeaker so that a tape recording of a mouse moving through leaves could be broadcast from under the mouse. He then taped the loudspeaker to a board and covered the board with clay so that the owl would leave its footprints when it struck. If he turned on the recording and dragged the board along the floor, the owl never missed. Apparently, it could adjust to the changing position of the sound as it flew.

To be sure the owl heard no noise during its flight, he attached a wire to the owl's perch. The recording would be turned off as soon as the owl took off from the perch. The owl would have to depend on its ability to locate the mouse by the sound it heard just before starting its flight. By marking the positions of the owl's perch and the points where it landed, Payne found that for distances of up to 7 m (23 ft), the owl never missed the mouse by more than one degree (see Figure 14). This means that its biggest error over a 7-m distance was never more than 12 cm (4.8 in). This is just about the size of the owl's outstretched claws.

[FIGURE 14]

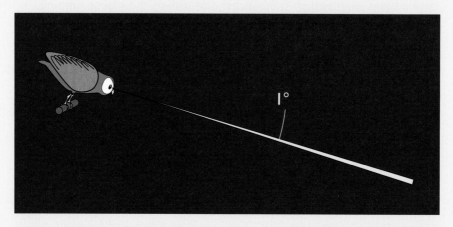

Within 7 m (23 ft), an owl never missed its prey by more than one degree, even in total darkness. At 7 m, an error of one degree is only 12 cm (4.8 in).

Interestingly, the owl seemed to know its limitations. If the sound made by the "mouse" was more than 7 m away, the owl would land slightly short of the mouse and then wait until it heard another sound before pouncing.

To find out how an owl strikes its prey, Payne took movies. First, he filmed an owl with the lights on. His movies showed that after an owl heard the mouse, it turned to face the sound, leaned its head forward, and pushed off from its perch. The owl made one stroke of its wings and then glided straight to the mouse. As it approached its prey, the owl suddenly moved its feet forward from beneath its tail to a point under its chin. Then, just before striking, it pulled its head back and spread its claws.

Because humans have more difficulty walking a straight line in darkness than in light, Payne thought an owl might strike differently in darkness than in light. To film his owl in darkness, he used a sniper-scope. A sniperscope is a device that can form images of objects from the infrared light (heat) they emit. The images appear on a screen similar to a small television screen. A movie camera can be used to take pictures of the screen every 1/24 second. Payne found that in darkness the owl flapped its wings several times, flew more slowly than in light, and swung its feet back and forth as it moved.

Payne reasoned that the owl on its perch hears the sound coming along a different path than the path its feet must follow to reach the mouse. Figure 15a shows how the two paths differ. To place its ears and feet along the same path leading to the prey, the owl leans forward to hear the sound. This places the bird's ears and feet on the same straight-line path to the mouse (see Figure 15b). Just before it strikes, the owl swings its feet forward and its head back. This places its feet along the path its ears were following and its ears back where its feet were.

An owl's foot has four talons that cover a rectangular area (see Figure 16). To grasp a mouse most effectively, the owl should be moving across the mouse's path when it strikes (see Figure 17) so that its claws reach across the mouse's back. Payne's movies showed that the owl would often turn 90 degrees just before striking the mouse. And it would do this even in darkness. But how can an owl in total darkness know which way a mouse is facing?

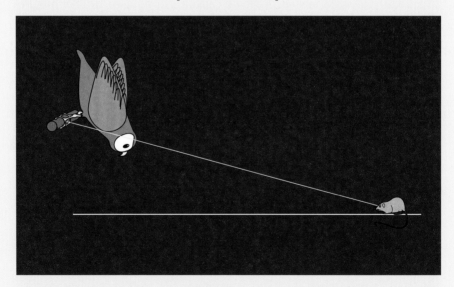

15a) The top line shows the straight-line path from the owl's ear to the mouse. The lower line shows the straight-line path from the owl's feet to the mouse. b) By leaning forward to listen just before it leaves its perch, the owl places its ears and feet on the same path to the mouse.

[FIGURE 16]

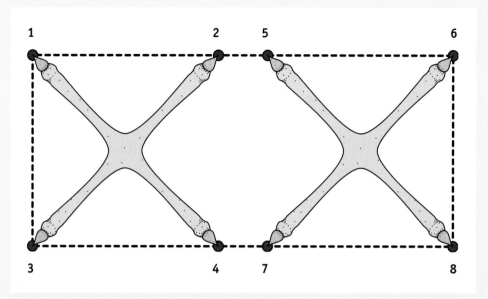

1 2 5 6

3 4 7 8

When an owl strikes, the tips of its talons are at the numbered positions shown in the drawing. Roger Payne discovered this pattern by placing a piece of black paper over the loudspeaker he used to send mouse sounds to the owl. When the owl struck, it left holes in the paper. Holes 1, 2, 3, and 4 were made by the owl's left foot. Holes 5, 6, 7, and 8 were made by the bird's right foot.

Perhaps the owl, using its keen sense of hearing, can tell the direction in which the mouse is moving. If it knows which way the mouse is moving, it knows which way the mouse's body is pointed. To test this idea, Payne used a string to drag a dead mouse along the floor of the totally dark room. He pulled the mouse in different directions. If the mouse was not moving across (perpendicular to) the owl's flight path, the owl would turn just before it struck until it was perpendicular to the path of the mouse.

To be sure the owl was guided by its ears and not its eyes, Payne dragged the mouse sideways, not headfirst, across the floor. The owl still pounced on its prey perpendicular to the direction the mouse was moving, even though this was now the worst angle of attack. The owl still "assumed" the mouse's head would be pointed in the direction it was traveling.

[FIGURE 17]

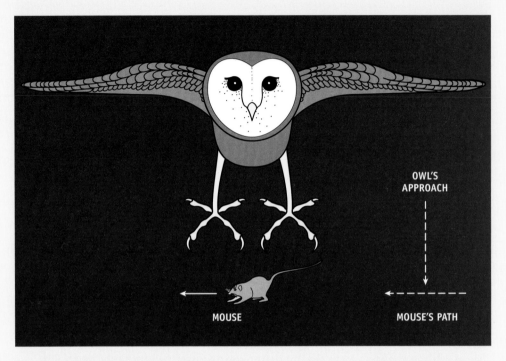

An owl is most successful in capturing its prey if it is perpendicular to the mouse's path when it strikes. Its talons will then completely surround the mouse's body.

Payne wondered if an owl in darkness can judge the distance to its prey with its ears. The fact that it extended its feet just before striking suggested that it can. But because the owl moved more slowly in darkness, flapped its wings, and kept its feet swinging beneath its body, Payne reasoned that it might not know the exact distance to its prey. Perhaps it was judging distance to the floor by the amount of back pressure created by the air it pushed downward with its wings. Perhaps it could tell when it was very close to its prey by smelling it. However, the fact that it would strike a loudspeaker indicated that it did not use its sense of smell. What kind of experiment do you think Payne devised to find out whether an owl can judge distance, not just direction, with its ears?

3.1 Using Your Ears to Find Direction

Materials:

-tape measure

-masking tape

-marking pen

-rubber tubing about 1.5 m (5 ft) long (old piece of garden hose works well)

-a friend

-small stick

-two spoons

-string

-chair

-large room

-blindfold (towel will do)

In one of his experiments, Roger Payne plugged one of the owl's ears with cotton. You may have wondered why plugging only one ear with cotton prevented the owl from locating the mouse. This experiment will help you to understand why an owl needs both ears to find a mouse in darkness.

You can locate objects in space with your own ears. Distant sounds are fainter than sounds that are nearby. Sounds to the left of center reach your left ear slightly before they reach your right ear. Similarly, sounds to the right of center reach your right ear slightly before they reach your left ear. This difference in time for sound to reach your left and right ears allows you to judge the direction from which the sound is coming.

You can easily demonstrate that the difference in time for sound to reach your two ears allows you to determine the sound's direction. Use a tape measure and a piece of masking tape or a marking pen to mark the center of a piece of rubber tubing about 1.5 m (5 ft) long. Place the tubing behind a friend and ask him or her to hold the ends of the tube in his or her ears, as shown in Figure 18. Use a small stick to scratch the tube to the right or left of the center line that you marked. Can your friend tell which ear is closer to the point where the scratch was made? How far to the right of center must the scratch be made before your friend can tell that the sound is coming from the right? How far to the left of center must the scratch be made before your friend can tell that the sound is coming from the left?

To see that someone can determine direction with his or her ears, hold the end of the handle of a spoon. Use a second spoon to strike this spoon. The spoons will serve as your source of sound in this experiment.

Place a chair in the center of a large room. Ask a friend to sit on the chair. Explain that you are going to test his or her ability to determine the direction of sound, and that you need to apply a blindfold.

After covering your friend's eyes, be sure that he or she cannot see. Be sure, too, that your friend is facing directly forward. Then use the spoons to generate a sound several meters (yards) directly in front of your friend, as shown in Figure 19. Ask your friend to point to the direction where he or she thinks the sound was made.

Next, generate sounds from a number of different positions to the right and left of your friend. How accurately can he or she identify the location of the sounds you make? You might like to mark the position of the sound and the direction your friend points with small pieces of tape on the floor. Label the two corresponding pieces of tape with the same number, and an S (for Sound) or P (for Pointing). Use different pieces of tape and different numbers for each trial.

Is your friend able to locate sounds best if they come from directly in front? from the left of center? from the right of center? from behind? from the side?

Does the distance to the sound affect your friend's ability to locate its direction?

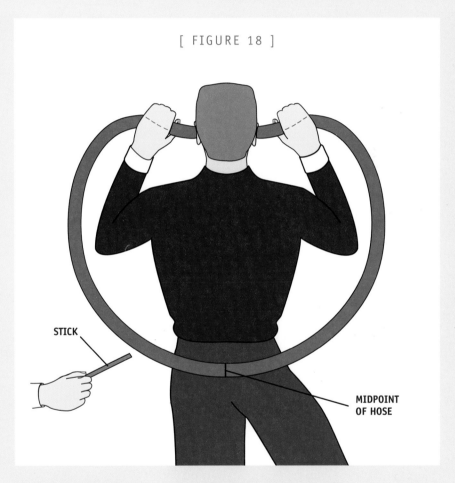

[FIGURE 18]

STICK

MIDPOINT
OF HOSE

Sound travels along the air in a hose. Can you tell whether the scratch is made to the right or left of center of the hose?

[FIGURE 19]

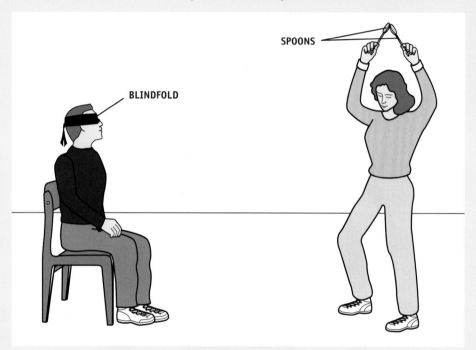

Can a person who is blindfolded tell the direction from which a sound comes?

Science Fair Project Idea

Is it just as easy for a friend to locate the direction of a different sound, such as one made by snapping your fingers? Design an experiment to investigate.

Materials:
- large empty room
- a friend
- small object
- blindfold (towel will do)
- short length of 2-in x 4-in board
- watch or clock with second hand
- paper and pencil
- calculator (optional)

Roger Payne knew that humans have more difficulty walking a straight line in darkness than in light. He thought an owl might also strike differently in darkness than in light. He said this might be true if both owls and humans find it more difficult to keep their balance in darkness than in light.

Does darkness affect your ability to walk in a straight line? To find out, stand at one end of a large empty room. Have a friend place a small object at the base of the wall on the opposite side of the room. Then walk slowly along a straight-line path to the object, keeping your hands and arms stretched out in front of you. Have your friend stand behind you to judge the straightness of your walk. (The reason for keeping your hands and arms outstretched is to make the conditions the same when you walk in darkness. Then you will want to keep your arms and hands in front of you to avoid bumping into anything.)

Now repeat the experiment with a blindfold on. Your friend will again judge the straightness of your walk and warn you when you are approaching the opposite wall. Repeat this experiment several times. What do you conclude? Do you walk straighter in light than in darkness? What happens when your friend tries this experiment?

To compare your balance in darkness and light, place a short length of a 2-in x 4-in board on the floor. With your eyes open, place one foot on

[FIGURE 20]

**PIECE OF
2 X 4 LUMBER**

How long can you balance your body using only one foot on a piece of lumber? Can you do as well when you are blindfolded?

the board and raise your other foot, as shown in Figure 20. Have a friend use a watch or clock with a second hand to measure and record the time that you can remain balanced on one foot. Repeat the experiment while balancing on your other foot. How long can you balance on this foot? Repeat the experiment three times. Determine the average length of time that you can balance on one foot.

Now repeat the experiment while wearing a blindfold. Determine the average length of time that you can balance on one foot with your eyes covered. Does darkness affect your ability to keep your balance?

 Science Fair Project Idea

You probably had trouble balancing and walking in a straight line with your eyes closed. Was your difficulty caused by darkness, or was it because your eyes were closed? Design your own experiment to find out.

Materials:
- rubber gloves
- owl pellets
- newspaper
- tweezers
- magnifying glass
- a field guide to mammals

As you know, some owls roost in barns. Others roost in trees, church steeples, or cemeteries. If you know a place where owls live, **get permission from an adult** to look around on the ground beneath their roosts. You will probably find matted, hairy, dark wads. These oval wads, called owl pellets, are about 5–8 cm (2–3 in) long and half as wide.

Owls have no teeth. They use their hooked beak to tear their food into pieces that they swallow whole. They cannot digest some parts of the material they swallow, such as hair, seed coats, bones, and insect skeletons. They cough up this undigested matter after the rest of their prey has been at least partially digested. It is the undigested material that makes up the pellets.

Wearing rubber gloves, collect some owl pellets and take them to your home or school. (If you can't find owl pellets, you can buy some from a science supply house that carries biological materials. Your teacher may have a catalog you can use.) Place the pellets on an old newspaper. With the rubber gloves on, use tweezers to pull the pellets apart. Unless very recently regurgitated, the pellets will be dry and odorless. Examine the material inside the pellet with a magnifying glass. Do you find bones? insect skeletons? seed coats?

A field guide to mammals will help you identify the animals from which the bones came. What does an owl eat? What adaptations do owls have to help them obtain the foods that make up their diet?

Science Fair Project Idea

Collect as many bones from a single owl pellet as possible. Try to reassemble a skeleton using the bones that fit together. Use a textbook to check bone structure and identify the type of animal skeleton you assembled. Glue the bones together onto a piece of cardboard.

Chapter 4

More Investigations of Animal Behavior

IN THIS CHAPTER YOU WILL EXAMINE THE BEHAVIOR OF SOME COMMON SMALL ANIMALS, AS WELL AS A LARGER ANIMAL—SQUIRRELS. You will start with animals whose behavior is mostly innate. One general rule to follow when working with animals is this: Don't do anything to an animal that you wouldn't do to yourself.

Materials:

- sow bugs
- paper cup
- sand
- peat moss
- cardboard
- 2 deep plastic containers, about 30 cm (12 in) on a side

- moist sponge
- raw potato
- 3 large jar tops
- black construction paper
- lighted place that is not hot

Sow bugs (pill bugs, or wood lice), like the one shown in Figure 21, can be found in damp places. Look under stones, logs, and leaves, where they feed on decaying plants. Collect some sow bugs (about 3 dozen) in a paper cup. Place a mixture of sand and damp peat moss in a plastic container (about 30 cm [12 in] on a side), then put the sow bugs on the soil. Add a moist sponge to the container, and put a cardboard cover over it. About once a week, add a piece of raw potato.

To find out the kind of environment that sow bugs prefer, cover the bottom of another plastic container with sand. Push three large jar tops into the sand with their open ends up. The open tops should be level with the sand, but empty. Place dry peat moss in one jar top, moist peat moss in the second, and wet peat moss in the third. Cover half of each jar top with black construction paper, as shown in Figure 22. Place about 20 sow bugs on the sand, and put the container in a lighted but not hot place, because sow bugs will die in hot sunlight. A bright basement; a cool, lighted garage; or a shady place would work well.

[FIGURE 21]

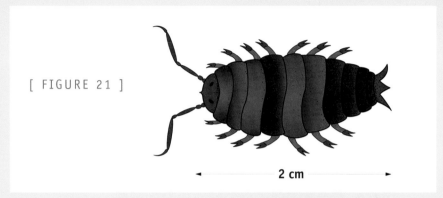

2 cm

Sow bugs, like the one shown here, are very common. You might find some in your basement or under a rock.

[FIGURE 22]

Do sow bugs prefer a dry, damp, or wet environment? Do they prefer light or darkness?

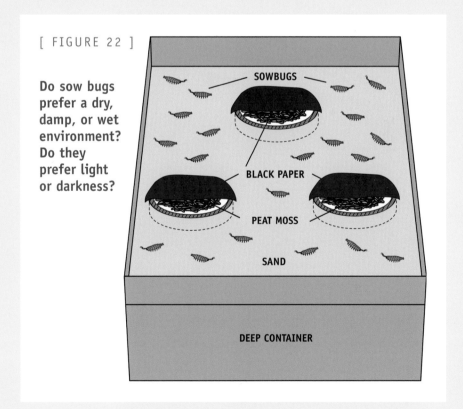

SOWBUGS

BLACK PAPER

PEAT MOSS

SAND

DEEP CONTAINER

The next day, look for the sow bugs. Are they still wandering around on the sand, or have some of them chosen one of the three peat-moss environments? Can you tell which environment they prefer? Do they prefer light or darkness?

Science Fair Project Idea

Design experiments of your own to find out what kind of temperature (cold, cool, or warm) sow bugs prefer. Can sow bugs smell? Do they respond to touch? Can they hear? Can they learn?

Materials:

- earthworms
- shovel
- Styrofoam cup
- soil
- large shoe box
- cardboard
- scissors
- tape
- clear plastic wrap
- red cellophane or clear red plastic
- paper towels
- cardboard box, about 30 cm (12 in) long, wide, and deep
- dry sand
- damp sand
- dry soil
- damp soil
- dry leaves
- damp leaves
- spoon

Find about a dozen earthworms by digging in moist soil. Place the worms in a large Styrofoam cup that holds some soil.

Divide a large shoe box into three parts by taping pieces of cardboard across the box, as shown in Figure 23. The cardboard dividers should not touch the bottom of the box. Leave about a 3-cm (1-in) gap between the cardboard and the bottom of the box so that the worms can crawl under the cardboard. Use scissors to cut square openings in the lid about 8 cm (3 in) on a side above each of the two end compartments.

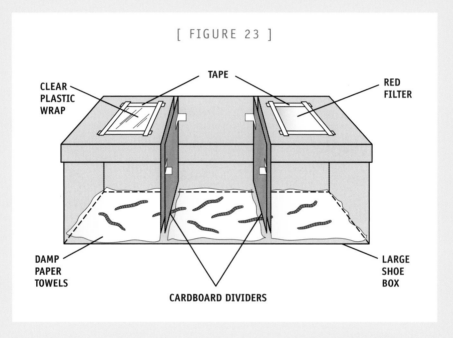

[FIGURE 23]

CLEAR
PLASTIC
WRAP

TAPE

RED
FILTER

DAMP
PAPER
TOWELS

CARDBOARD DIVIDERS

LARGE
SHOE
BOX

Do earthworms prefer light or darkness, and how do they respond to
red light?

Tape clear plastic wrap over one opening and several layers of red cellophane or clear red plastic over the other opening. Cover the bottom of the box with moist paper towels. Then put a few earthworms in each compartment. Place the box near a window so that light can enter the two end compartments. Where are the earthworms after several hours? Are they still evenly distributed among the three compartments, or are more in one compartment than another?

Is there any evidence that earthworms respond to light? If there is, do they seem to be attracted to light or repelled by it? Do they respond differently to red light than to ordinary sunlight? Design an experiment to see if earthworms respond to green or blue light.

Use pieces of cardboard to divide a cardboard box into six sections. The dividers should touch the bottom of the box, but they should be only about two-thirds as high as the box (see Figure 24). Into these six sections, place dry sand, damp sand, dry soil, damp soil, dry leaves, and damp leaves. Be sure the sections are full so that when you put about a dozen earthworms in the box, they can crawl along the tops of the different kinds of material and choose the one they want to stay in. Cover the box.

After a day, open the box and use a spoon to carefully remove the sand, soil, and leaves from the different compartments. Record the number of earthworms in each type of material. Do earthworms like to live in a dry or a damp environment? Which do they seem to like best— sand, soil, or leaves?

When you have finished your experiments, return the earthworms to the same place where you dug them up.

[FIGURE 24]

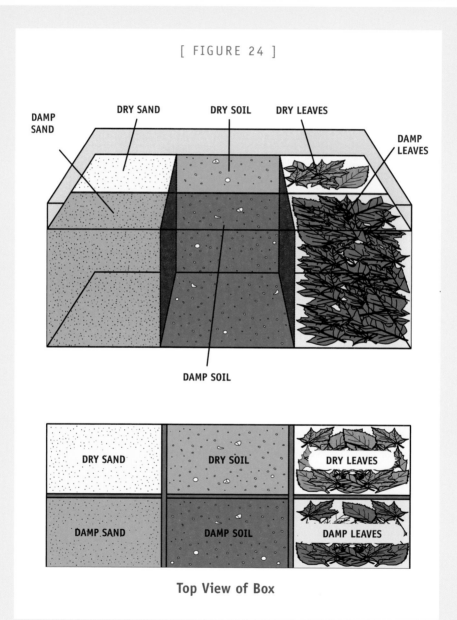

DAMP
SAND

DRY SAND

DRY SOIL

DRY LEAVES

DAMP
LEAVES

DAMP SOIL

DRY SAND

DRY SOIL

DRY LEAVES

DAMP SAND

DAMP SOIL

DAMP LEAVES

Top View of Box

Do earthworms prefer dry or damp soil? Which do they like to live in: sand, soil, or dead leaves?

Science Fair Project Ideas

- Which environment do you think earthworms would prefer: the environment you have found they like best, or an environment of oatmeal? Design an experiment to find out.
- Design an experiment to discover whether earthworms prefer wet soil or damp soil.
- Will earthworms react to vinegar? to ammonia? To find out, place several earthworms on moist paper towels in a box. Dip a cotton swab on a stick into some vinegar. Then hold the wet cotton near (not touching) an earthworm's head and wait. Does the worm react? Do other earthworms react to the vinegar? Do they react to a cotton swab soaked in an ammonia solution? If they react, do you think they react by smelling or by touching the chemical?

Materials:

- mealworms (several dozen) obtained from a local pet store
- small glass, plastic, or metal container
- bran or dry cereal, such as bran flakes, corn flakes, or wheat flakes
- paper towel
- potato or apple
- cardboard shoe box
- clear plastic tape
- mirror, or a sheet of clear rigid plastic
- clock or watch
- small glass jar such as a baby food jar
- refrigerator
- white paper

- magnifying glass
- ruler
- cardboard
- paper drinking straw
- table
- talcum powder
- flashlight
- cotton swabs
- vinegar
- ammonia solution (sold in stores as ammonia cleaner)
- water
- pencil or toothpick
- paper of several different colors
- scissors
- paper with a pattern

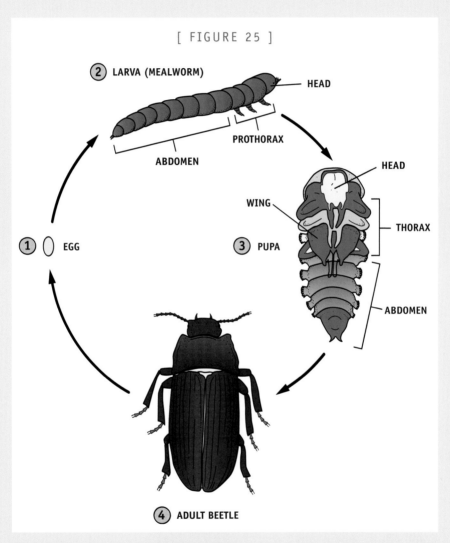

[FIGURE 25]

② LARVA (MEALWORM)

HEAD

PROTHORAX

ABDOMEN

HEAD

WING

THORAX

① ◯ EGG

③ PUPA

ABDOMEN

④ ADULT BEETLE

Mealworms (Tenebrio molitor) are the larval stage of the grain beetle.
The life cycle of a mealworm includes four distinct stages: egg, larva
(mealworm), pupa, and adult (beetle).

Like many insects, the grain beetle (*Tenebrio molitor*) passes through four distinct stages in its life cycle, as shown in Figure 25. Mealworms are the larval stage of this beetle. The larval stage lasts about four months. The mealworm then goes into a resting (pupal) stage for about two weeks before the adult beetle emerges. The adults live for several months, and each female will lay about 500 eggs before she dies. These eggs hatch into mealworms in about a week. Mealworms are useful for experiments because they are easy to care for, they are inexpensive, and their eggs hatch quickly.

For your experiments, you will need several dozen mealworms. You can buy them from a local pet store or from a biological supply house. The worms will live nicely in a small glass, plastic, or metal container (see Figure 26). Put a handful of bran or dry cereal, such as bran flakes, corn flakes, or wheat flakes, into the container. Cover the food with a paper towel. Put a piece of fresh potato or apple on the towel. The fresh food will provide all the water the mealworms need.

If you would like to watch the life cycle of these beetles, simply change the food supply when the bran or cereal flakes become powdery. Occasionally add fresh pieces of potato or apple to provide moisture.

GENERAL BEHAVIOR OF MEALWORMS

Put about 20 of your mealworms in a cardboard shoe box. A strip of clear tape around the top edge of the box will cause them to slip back if they try to crawl out. Watch the mealworms for a while. Notice their tendency to move along walls and around corners.

To see how mealworms move, place one on a mirror or a sheet of clear rigid plastic. How many legs does the mealworm have? How do the legs move as the animal walks? How fast does it walk? How long would it take a mealworm to walk a mile?

Place one or two mealworms in a small glass jar. Put the jar in the refrigerator for a few minutes. The cold temperature will make the mealworms move more slowly, so they will be easier to observe. When the mealworms are sluggish, remove them from the refrigerator. Put them on a

[FIGURE 26]

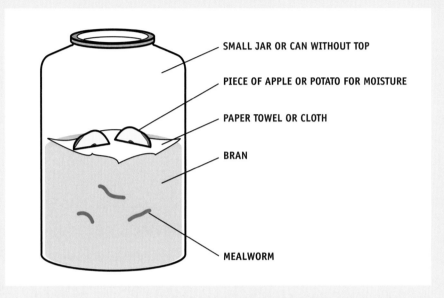

SMALL JAR OR CAN WITHOUT TOP

PIECE OF APPLE OR POTATO FOR MOISTURE

PAPER TOWEL OR CLOTH

BRAN

MEALWORM

Set up a jar or can in which to keep and nurture mealworms.

piece of white paper and examine them closely with a magnifying glass. How big are they? How wide? How many segments make up their bodies? Can you find their eyes? Their antennae? Their mouthparts? What do their legs look like? Do they have fine hairs on their bodies? If so, what might these be used for?

Place a mealworm at the center of a small sheet of cardboard. Raise one side of the cardboard so that the mealworm is on an inclined plane. Which way does the mealworm move? Repeat the experiment with the cardboard at different angles of incline. Does the mealworm always move the same way? Is the mealworm's movement affected by the angle of the incline?

Put a paper drinking straw on a table. Place a mealworm headfirst into the drinking straw. What does the mealworm do? What happens if you place the mealworm into the straw tail first?

HOW DO MEALWORMS FIND FOOD?

Try to discover how mealworms detect food. Do they see it, do they smell it, or do they just bump into it by accident? To find out, cover the bottom of the shoe box with a very fine layer of talcum powder. The worms will leave tracks in the powder when they move. Place a small pile of bran or dry cereal flakes near the center of the box. Then put about a dozen mealworms at one end of the box. After the worms have found the food, examine the paths they followed. How do you think they found the food? Do you think they would find the food sooner if you put the food near a wall?

HOW CAN YOU MAKE A MEALWORM BACK UP?

Mealworms sometimes move backward. What stimuli might make a mealworm move backward? Here are a few to try. You may be able to think of some others. Try each stimulus many times with different mealworms.

- Shine a flashlight at the mealworm. If the worm backs up, is it because of the light or the flashlight itself? How can you find out?

- Dip a cotton swab into vinegar. Hold it in front of the mealworm. Repeat the experiment using ammonia water. Repeat once more with water.

- Touch the mealworm gently with a pencil or a toothpick. What happens? Does it matter where you touch the animal?

- Make a loud noise near the mealworm.

- Blow air through a drinking straw at the mealworm. What happens? Does it matter where the air hits the mealworm?

- Block a worm's path with different kinds of material.

    Which stimulus works best? Is there any stimulus that works the same way every time?

DO MEALWORMS HAVE A FAVORITE COLOR?

Put four papers of different colors on the floor of a cardboard shoe box. Place a white paper circle in the center of the box, as shown in Figure 27. Put a few mealworms on the white circle. Do they seem to have a preference for one color? What evidence do you have?

Design an experiment to see if mealworms prefer paper with a pattern as opposed to plain paper.

[FIGURE 27]

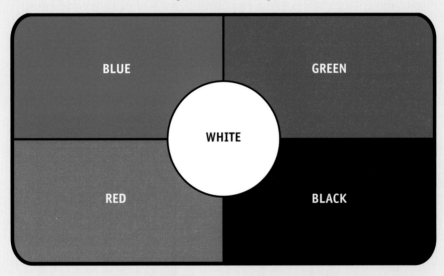

Do mealworms have a favorite color?

MEALWORMS IN MAZES

You can cut and bend cardboard to make walls inside a shoe box. Place the walls so as to make T-mazes, such as those shown in Figure 28. (Why do you think they are called T-mazes?) As you can see, the maze in Figure 28a forces the worm to make a left turn in order to reach the food at the end of the maze. The maze in Figure 28b forces the worm to make a right turn.

Does forcing a worm to turn right or left at the start of the maze affect the way it will turn (right or left) when given a choice at the end of the maze?

Does the length the worm has to crawl after the forced turn affect the direction it turns at the end of the maze?

CLEAN UP

You might like to keep mealworms and watch them go through the pupal and adult stages of their life cycle. When you are finished with the mealworms, place them outside near a rock, under which they can crawl.

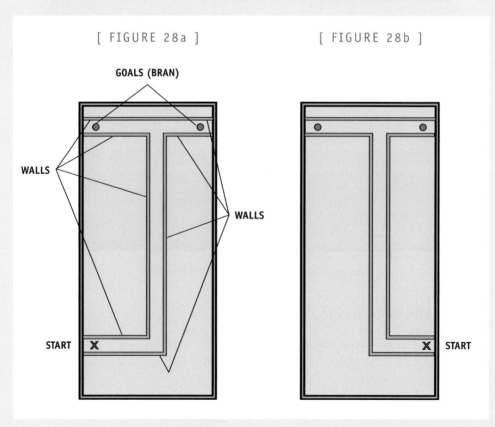

Mealworm Mazes with Forced Turns

Science Fair Project Ideas

- Design experiments to find out how temperature, type of food, moisture, and other factors affect the length of the beetle's life cycle.
- Design a variety of mealworm mazes. What can you learn about mealworm behavior from these mazes?
- Design experiments to answer one or more of the following questions:

  1. Can mealworms see?
  2. Will mealworms crawl over the edge of a table and fall, or will they stay along the table's edge?
  3. Can mealworms hear?
  4. Mealworms are often seen crawling along walls. How do they find a wall? How do they sense that the wall is there?
  5. Do mealworms prefer light or darkness?
  6. What food do mealworms like best?
  7. Do mealworms prefer a dry or a moist environment?
  8. Do mealworms have a preference with respect to the surface over which they crawl? You might try shiny paper, silk, sandpaper, newspaper, felt, and wood. What do you find?

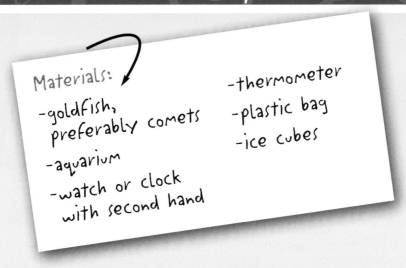

Materials:
- goldfish, preferably comets
- aquarium
- watch or clock with second hand
- thermometer
- plastic bag
- ice cubes

Fish live in water, so they don't breathe air. They obtain their oxygen from the small amount of the gas that is dissolved in water. If you watch a fish closely, you will see that it appears to gulp water. But the fish doesn't swallow the water. Instead, the water passes over its gills (see Figure 29). The oxygen in the water enters the blood through the gills. This is similar to the way oxygen passes from air to blood in your lungs.

Unlike you, a fish is cold–blooded. Its body temperature falls when the water it is in cools. To see if temperature affects a fish's gulping (respiration) rate, measure a goldfish's gulping rate in its aquarium. Count the number of times it gulps in 30 seconds. Do this several times and take an average.

Use a thermometer to measure the temperature of the water in the aquarium. Then let a plastic bag filled with ice cubes float in the aquarium. When the temperature of the water has fallen 5 degrees Celsius (about 10 degrees Fahrenheit), remove the bag of ice. Again count how many times the same goldfish gulps in 30 seconds. Maintain the lower temperature and count the respiration for several 30-second intervals, then take an average. How does temperature affect a goldfish's respiration?

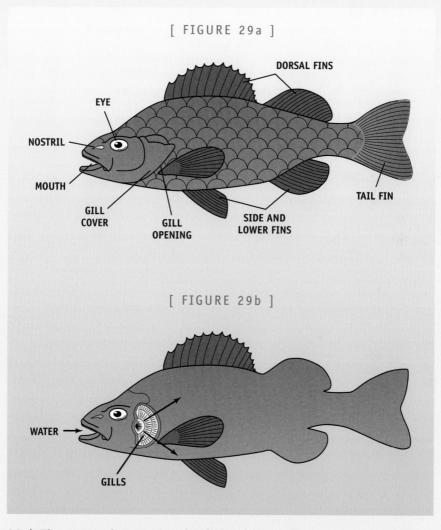

[FIGURE 29a]

DORSAL FINS

EYE

NOSTRIL

MOUTH

GILL
COVER

GILL
OPENING

SIDE AND
LOWER FINS

TAIL FIN

[FIGURE 29b]

WATER

GILLS

29a) The external anatomy of a fish. b) The gills lie under the gill cover. As water enters the fish's mouth and flows over the many tiny blood vessels in the gills, oxygen passes from the water to the fish's blood. The water then flows out of the fish's body through the gill openings, one on each side of its head.

Science Fair Project Idea

Design your own experiments to answer the following questions: Do goldfish sleep? Can goldfish hear? Do goldfish prefer light or darkness? Can a goldfish be made to swim upside down? Does temperature affect a person's breathing rate?

4.5 Building Bird Feeders to Outwit Squirrels

Materials:
-birdseed
-squirrels (in a yard or park)
-materials to make a "squirrelproof" bird feeder

If you have a bird feeder, you may know that squirrels enjoy feasting on the seeds you put out for birds. Try to design a bird feeder that you think is "squirrelproof." Watch the squirrels and record your observations. Use your observations to try to answer the following questions:

Can the squirrels find a way to get to the bird feeder? How do they proceed? Do you think they learn? If they learn, do they learn by trial and error? Or do they learn by insight or thinking? What makes you think so?

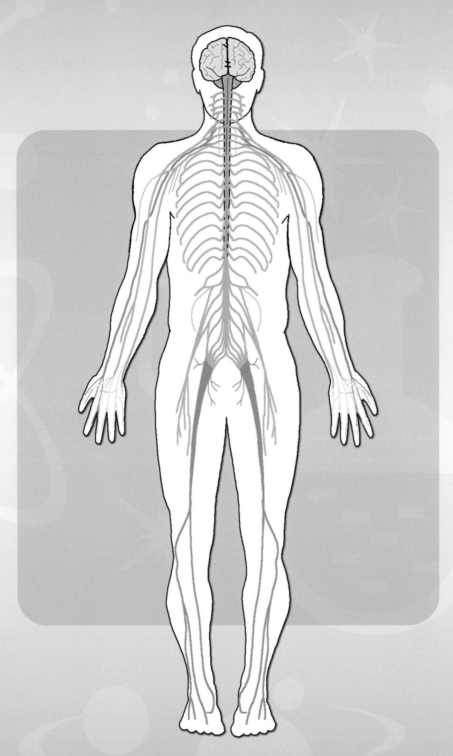

Scientists study the human nervous system, which includes the brain, spinal cord, and nerves.

Chapter 5

Studying Human Behavior

THE WORD *PSYCHOLOGY* IS DERIVED FROM THE GREEK WORD *PSYCHE*, WHICH MEANS "SOUL." But psychology has come to mean "the study of behavior." Human behavior is difficult to understand because it involves both biology and social interactions. Psychology is therefore regarded as a biosocial science.

The human nervous system responds to stimuli, outside agents that create an action. For instance, a crack of thunder causes our ears to hear. However, what we sense and the way we respond are influenced by the setting in which we grew up. Unlocking the secrets of the human mind has been the focus of countless science experiments, dating back to the time of Aristotle.

Over 150 years ago, physiologists (scientists who study life processes) conducted some of the first psychology experiments documented in modern medical history. Physiologists were trying to measure, or estimate, the speed at which nerve impulses travel in the human body. By measuring reaction time—the time it takes for a person to respond to an outside agent—they could estimate the time it takes an impulse to travel from the eye to the brain and then to the hand.

In the first two experiments of this chapter, you will measure reaction time first using a visual stimulus, and next using a sound stimulus. In Experiment 5.3 you will discover, as did nineteenth-century scientists, that we are limited in our ability to distinguish the intensity of one stimulus from another. The fourth experiment will allow you to investigate whether or not colors affect emotions. Finally, in the last experiment, you will examine how what you see influences what you smell.

Materials:
- yardstick
- Table 1
- a friend
- paper and pencil

You can carry out an experiment designed to measure a human's reaction time: the speed of response to an outside stimulus.

First, find a smooth wall that will not be harmed by a few fingerprints, perhaps in the kitchen. Place a yardstick against the wall with the zero end down and the other end slightly above your head. Stand to one side of the yardstick and place one thumb against the yardstick at about the ten-inch mark, as shown in Figure 30. Keep the rest of your hand flat against the wall.

Ask a friend to be your subject in this experiment. Have your subject stand in front of the yardstick with her preferred hand flat against the wall, thumb raised slightly above the yardstick's surface just below the 2-inch mark. The subject can stop the fall of the yardstick by moving her thumb quickly toward the wall.

To begin the experiment, say to the subject, "Watch my thumb, which is pressing the yardstick against the wall. When I move that thumb up to release the yardstick, move your thumb against the yardstick and stop its fall. A few seconds before I release the yardstick, I will say, 'Get ready.' At that point, watch my thumb closely. When you see it move, move your thumb as quickly as you can to stop the yardstick. Then wait for me to record the distance it fell."

Repeat the experiment five times. Each time wait between one and five seconds after you say "Get ready" before raising your thumb to release the yardstick so that the subject cannot anticipate the release. If the subject does try to anticipate your release, start over; that is, do five more trials.

Record the distance the yardstick falls after each trial by subtracting 2 inches (the initial position of the subject's thumb) from the number of inches (including fractions) just above the final position of the subject's thumb. Then calculate the average distance it fell over the five trials. Table 1 tells you how long it takes, in hundredths of a second, for a

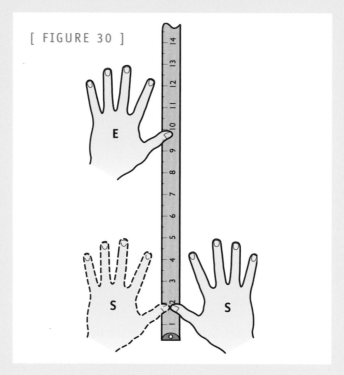

[FIGURE 30]

The position of hands of the experimenter (E) and subject (S) over a yardstick. The drawing assumes the subject is right-handed. Left-handed subjects should use their left hand. The subject will use both hands during the third part of the experiment.

yardstick to fall certain distances. You can use the average distance the yardstick fell to find the subject's reaction time.

What reaction time will you record in your notebook if the yardstick fell 11 inches?

What reaction time should you record if the yardstick fell 20½ inches?

Repeat the entire experiment, but this time you will be the subject and your subject will be the experimenter.

Based on the results of both experiments, estimate, in inches per second, the speed at which nerve impulses travel in the human body.

TABLE 1.

The time for an object to fall each of the distances shown. Times have been rounded to the nearest hundredths of a second. (in = inches; s = seconds.)

Distance the yardstick fell (in)	Time to fall this distance (s)
1.0	0.07
2.0	0.10
3.0	0.13
4.0	0.14
5.0	0.16
6.0	0.18
8.0	0.20
10.0	0.23
12.0	0.25
14.0	0.27
16.0	0.29
18.0	0.31
20.0	0.32
22.0	0.34
24.0	0.35
28.0	0.38
32.0	0.41

After completing the next two parts of this experiment, you will have enough data to make an analysis and draw some conclusions about reaction time.

REACTION TIME INVOLVING DISCRIMINATION

In the second part of this experiment, the subject must discriminate—make a judgment—between two stimuli. In releasing the yardstick, you, as the experimenter, will lift either your thumb or your index finger. If you raise your index finger, the yardstick will not fall. If you raise your thumb, the yardstick will fall as it did in the first part of this experiment. The subject will now have to watch both your thumb and index finger and make a decision based on the stimulus presented.

Record the distance the yardstick falls after each trial in which you lift your thumb. (Obviously, there can be no determination of reaction time if the yardstick does not fall.) Calculate the average distance it fell over five trials. Use Table 1, as before, to determine the subject's reaction time.

Switch roles with your subject and repeat the second part of the experiment.

REACTION TIME INVOLVING A CHOICE

In the third part of this experiment, the subject has to make a choice between two responses. In releasing the yardstick, you will either lift your thumb straight toward the subject or toward your index finger. The subject will now have both thumbs raised just below the 2-inch mark (as shown by the dotted-line hand and the solid-line hand in Figure 30).

Tell your subject to use his or her left thumb to stop the yardstick when your thumb is raised toward him or her, and his or her right thumb to stop the yardstick when you move your thumb toward your index finger.

Again, repeat the experiment five times and record the distance the yardstick falls after each trial. (If the subject uses the wrong thumb, start over; that is, do five more trials.) Then calculate the average distance the yardstick fell over the five valid trials. Using Table 1, determine the subject's average reaction time.

Switch roles with your subject and repeat the third part of this experiment.

How do the reaction times for the first, second, and third parts of the experiment compare? Is there any significant difference in reaction time if the subject has to discriminate between two different stimuli as in the second part of the experiment? Is there any significant difference in reaction time if the subject has to make a choice between responses as in the third part of the experiment? If there are differences in reaction time under these three conditions, can you explain what the cause might be?

 Science Fair Project Ideas

- Repeat this experiment with a number of different subjects. Does reaction time seem to be related to a subject's age? To a subject's gender? To a subject's arm length? To a subject's athletic ability?
- Design and conduct an experiment to test reaction time when a subject has to discriminate among three stimuli. Design another experiment to test reaction time when a subject has to choose among three responses to three different stimuli. How does the number of alternative stimuli or responses affect the reaction time?

Materials:
-yardstick
-Table 1
-a friend

Repeat the first part of Experiment 5.1 using a sound stimulus in place of a visual stimulus. Have the subject close her eyes or blindfold her and tell her that you will say "Go!" at the moment you release the yardstick. Upon hearing this sound stimulus, the subject is to react as before and move her thumb as quickly as possible to stop the yardstick.

Repeat the experiment five times. For each trial, record the distance the yardstick falls. Then determine the average distance the yardstick fell and use Table 1 to determine the subject's average reaction time.

How does the reaction time to a sound stimulus compare to the reaction time for the visual stimulus you used in the first part of Experiment 5.1? Are they significantly different? That is, do they consistently differ by more than 0.05 to 0.1 seconds? If they do, can you explain?

 Science Fair Project Idea

Design an experiment to measure the reaction time to a touch stimulus. How does it compare with the reaction times to sound and to visual stimuli?

5.3 What Difference in Weight Is Noticeable?

Materials:
- very large can and very small can
- sand
- balance or scale
- several people to serve as subjects
- notebook
- pen or pencil
- blindfold
- table
- chair
- standard weights found in most science labs: 10 to 200 grams (g) in 10-g increments; 300 to 2,000 g in 100-g increments; and 50-g weight

Another early experiment about human behavior involved distinguishing a change in the intensity of a weight stimulus; in other words, deciding whether one object is heavier than another. You can do a very simple experiment to see how deceiving a weight stimulus can be.

Find a very large can and a very small can. Add sand to the small can until its weight is the same as that of the large empty can. Now ask someone to lift both cans, one at a time. Which can do they think is heavier? Can you explain why they think one can is heavier than the other?

Next, test people to find the "just noticeable difference" in weight that they can detect. To do this, blindfold a subject seated at a table. Ask the subject to keep his elbow on the table as he lifts a 100-gram weight, the handle of which you place between his thumb and first two fingers. The 100-gram weight will serve as the standard. Have the subject lift the standard. Then, after a five-second wait, have him lift a second weight for comparison. For comparison weights use 10, 20, 30, 40, 50,

60, 70, 80, 90, 110, 120, 130, 140, 150, 160, 170, 180, 190, and 200 grams (g).

After the second in each pair of lifts, ask the subject whether the second weight is lighter, heavier, or the same weight as the standard. Record each response and the comparison weight. What is the smallest difference in weight the subject can detect? Is it the same for weights greater than 100 g as it is for weights less than 100 g?

Now repeat the experiment using 1,000 g (1 kg) as the standard weight. For comparison weights, use 100, 200, 300, 400, 500, 600, 700, 800, 900, 950, 1,050, 1,100, 1,200, 1,300, 1,400, 1,500, 1,600, 1,700, 1,800, 1,900, and 2,000 grams.

Record each response and the comparison weight. What is the smallest difference in weight the subject can detect? Is it the same for weights greater than 1,000 g as it is for weights less than 1,000 g?

Repeat the experiment with several different subjects.

How does the just noticeable difference for the heavier weights compare with the just noticeable difference for the lighter weights? How does the ratio of the just noticeable difference to the standard weight compare for the 100 g and the 1,000 g standard weights? Can you draw any conclusions regarding these differences?

5.4 What Is the Effect of Color on Human Emotion?

Materials:
- people to interview and observe
- pad of paper and pencil
- television set
- telephone

COLORED EMOTIONS

Do colors affect our emotions? We certainly respond to colors. A red light tells us to stop. A green light tells us it is safe to go. A yellow light warns us to be cautious. But what emotions, thoughts, or actions do we associate with colors? Do different people respond to colors in the same or different ways?

To find out, interview as many people as possible. Ask, "What do the following colors mean to you?" Then ask them to respond for each color listed in the chart below. Then ask, "How do the following colors make you feel (sad, angry, happy, sleepy, etc.)?" Record their answers in a chart like the one shown.

Do people respond in similar or different ways to a particular color? Does age affect their responses? Do men and boys respond differently than women and girls?

NAME OF PERSON	COLOR						
	White	Black	Blue	Green	Yellow	Orange	Red

DO NOT WRITE IN THIS BOOK

BODY LANGUAGE

You can often tell how people feel just by watching them. A yawn may indicate that someone is bored or tired. A smile may indicate happiness, or it may be a conditioned response to meeting someone new. Other actions might include shrugging, looking away, laughing, frowning, shouting, or sticking out a tongue.

Study people as you sit down at your family dinner table. Can you tell by looking whether someone is happy, sad, angry, bored, or annoyed? Do their words later confirm what you thought by just looking?

People usually use body language when they are responding to another person, an object, or a situation. Try watching people in a library, store, airplane terminal, classroom, dinner table, or any place where you can observe them. Sit far enough away that you cannot hear what is said. Don't stare—unless you want to see how someone responds when you do!

As you "people watch," make a table of your observations. Record the action you see, the message you think it sends, the response (if any) of someone receiving the message, and the reply (if any) sent by the receiver. One example is given in the short chart below.

ACTION	MESSAGE	RESPONSE	RETURN MESSAGE
Smile	Hi, friend!	Smile	Good to see you too!

SILENT TELEVISION AND INVISIBLE PEOPLE

Turn off the volume on a television set and just watch the people in a television movie. Can you tell how they feel about one another? If you can, what clues are you using?

Can you tell what the movie is about just by watching? If you can, what signs are helping you to understand the story?

When you talk on the telephone, you can't see the person with whom you are talking. What can you learn from the person's voice? Can you tell if he or she is happy? sad? angry? in a hurry? eager to talk?

Materials:
- a friend
- blindfold
- perfume
- table

Many animals, such as dogs, rely on their sense of smell more than their vision or hearing. To see how well you can use your own sense of smell, ask a friend to blindfold you. Then, while you wait, have your friend open a bottle of perfume and place it in an open place on a table near one side of a nearby room.

Your friend will then lead you into the room. Once there, you will try to locate the perfume by "following your nose." Your friend will warn you if you are about to bump into something—but you are to use only your sense of smell to find the perfume. Can your nose lead you to the perfume? How well can your friend do? Would you do better trying to find a ticking clock?

How else might you test your sense of smell?

Helen Keller, a famous woman who died in 1968, was both deaf and blind. She could readily identify people by their odor. To people who rely on their noses, instead of their eyes and ears as most of us do, a person's odor is as distinct as his or her appearance or voice.

 ## Science Fair Project Ideas

- Can you identify people by their odor? Design an experiment to find out.
- Design an experiment to find out if your sense of smell is better when you are blindfolded or in darkness than it is when you can see.
- Design another experiment to find out if your sense of hearing is better when you are blindfolded or in darkness than it is when you can see.

FURTHER READING

Books

Blair, Julianne Bochinski. *The Complete Workbook for Science Fair Projects.* Hoboken, N.J.: John Wiley & Sons, 2005.

Gerstein, Sherry. *The Most Extreme Animals.* Hoboken, N.J.: John Wiley & Sons, Inc., April, 2007.

Howell, Laura, Kirsteen Rogers, and Corinne Henderson. *The Usborne Internet-Linked Library of Science: Animal World.* London, England: Usborne Publishing Ltd., 2001.

_____. *Amazing Animals Q & A.* New York: Dorling Kindersley, Inc., 2007.

Moorman, Thomas. *How to Make Your Science Project Scientific.* Revised Edition. New York: John Wiley & Sons, Inc., 2002.

_____. *Planet Earth: Discover and Explore Wildlife Habitats, Animal Behavior, Conservation, and the Environment.* Minneapolis, Minn.: Two-Can Publishers, Inc., 2002.

Internet Addresses

Discovery Communications. *Animal Planet.* **2007.** http://animal.discovery.com/guides/atoz/atoz.html.

National Geographic Society. *National Geographic Kids.* **1996–2007.** http://kids.nationalgeographic.com/Animals/.

Sea World. *Animals.* **2007.** http://www.seaworld.org/animal-info/animal-bytes/index.htm.

INDEX